The Arc of Educational Change

The Arc of Educational Change

How the Collaboration of Philosophers, Activists, Teachers, and Policymakers Has Transformed Education

Donald Parkerson
Jo Ann Parkerson

ROWMAN & LITTLEFIELD
Lanham • Boulder • New York • London

Published by Rowman & Littlefield
An imprint of The Rowman & Littlefield Publishing Group, Inc.
4501 Forbes Boulevard, Suite 200, Lanham, Maryland 20706
www.rowman.com

86-90 Paul Street, London EC2A 4NE, United Kingdom

Copyright © 2023 by Donald Parkerson and Jo Ann Parkerson

All rights reserved. No part of this book may be reproduced in any form or by any electronic or mechanical means, including information storage and retrieval systems, without written permission from the publisher, except by a reviewer who may quote passages in a review.

British Library Cataloguing in Publication Information Available

Library of Congress Cataloging-in-Publication Data

Names: Parkerson, Donald Hugh, author. | Parkerson, Jo Ann, author.
Title: The arc of educational change: how the collaboration of philosophers, activists, teachers, and policymakers has transformed education / Donald Parkerson, Jo Ann Parkerson.
Description: Lanham, MD: Rowman & Littlefield, [2023] | Includes bibliographical references. | Summary: "This book takes a look at American educational history and focuses on the collaboration between teachers, policymakers, philosophers, and activists"—Provided by publisher.
Identifiers: LCCN 2022041979 (print) | LCCN 2022041980 (ebook) | ISBN 9781475864359 (cloth) | ISBN 9781475864366 (paperback) | ISBN 9781475864373 (epub)
Subjects: LCSH: Educational change—United States. | Education—Philosophy—United States. | Education—United States—History. | Education and state—United States.
Classification: LCC LB2806 .P357 2023 (print) | LCC LB2806 (ebook) | DDC 370.973—dc23/eng/20220930
LC record available at https://lccn.loc.gov/2022041979
LC ebook record available at https://lccn.loc.gov/2022041980

*To those who believe the arc of educational change
bends toward inclusion, equity, and justice*

Contents

Acknowledgments	ix
Introduction	xi
Chapter 1: The Foundationalists	1
Chapter 2: Advocates for the Poor	21
Chapter 3: Education for Democracy	37
Chapter 4: Gender Equity in Education	55
Chapter 5: The Common School	75
Chapter 6: A Curriculum for the Nation	93
Chapter 7: Freedmen's Bureau Schools	109
Chapter 8: The Progressives	127
Chapter 9: Champions of Racial Justice	149
Chapter 10: The Arc of Educational Change	171
References	187
About the Authors	193

Acknowledgments

We wish to thank our family, friends, and colleagues for their support and encouragement, especially Chris Oakley and Jennifer McKinnon, chairs of the History Department, East Carolina University; and Allison Danell, dean, Thomas Harriot College of Arts and Sciences. We also appreciate the kind endorsements of our book by professors Kenneth Wilburn and Heather Lyn Seibert. Tom Koerner, senior editor at Rowman & Littlefield, provided formative and thoughtful feedback, and the editorial and production staff were very helpful.

Introduction

COLLABORATION IN AMERICAN EDUCATIONAL HISTORY

At a time when individualism has come to dominate our world and we often celebrate the accomplishments of the great figures of the past and present, we sometimes forget that cooperation, collaboration, and networking have always been at the heart of progress, change, and improvement of our social order, our economy, and our educational system.

THE GREAT MAN THEORY

Examples of our adulation of the "great men" run through American history, presenting a simplistic vision of the past. In the field of American educational history, the veneration of a single individual at the expense of collaborative efforts of groups has been the focus of educational history for many years.

The Arc of Educational Change seeks to address this issue and place educational history into a more realistic, modern historical context. In an earlier era of American history, the veneration of such "great men" as founding fathers, inventors, industrialists, and financiers was seen as an act of patriotism. Today, however, we have a different, more inclusive vision of our world that strives to recognize individuals who traditionally have been excluded from our historical narrative. These include women, African Americans, immigrants, and working people. Moreover, as we recognize the interconnectedness of our social, political, and educational order, the focus on single individuals (especially the "great men" of the past) is inadequate, misdirected, and, frankly, outdated. *The Arc of Educational Change* provides a balance that recognizes the important role of individuals, as well as their collaborators, who helped promote positive educational change.

COLLABORATION THROUGH THE AGES

While our understanding of the importance of collaboration is often seen as a relatively new phenomenon in business, politics, and, of course, education, it is not. We have always cooperated and collaborated with one another. Communal fishing, hunting, religion, agriculture, and education have been the bedrock elements of our survival for millennia.

ORIGINS

But our emulation of a handful of "great men" in the past has obscured our understanding of the importance of that collaboration. For example, when Plutarch began to pen his famous *Parallel Lives* (sometimes referred to as *Plutarch's Lives*) in the first century CE, he created a new perspective on the writing of history. Moreover, his focus on the great men had a powerful influence on our emulation of singular individuals in the past and cemented the biography as the primary form of historical writing for centuries.

THE ARTS

In the field of art, Giorgio Vasari helped to strengthen the illusion of the lone genius artist. Vasari's *The Lives of the Artists*, written during the halcyon days of the Italian Renaissance in the sixteenth century, promoted the notion that such great artists as Leonardo DaVinci essentially were endowed with their amazing skills by God. This, of course, was a fundamental misunderstanding of the arts. For centuries, theater, dance, and music have relied on collaboration to promote artistic achievement. From the cooperative work that created early theater in Greece to the great operas and ballets of the Renaissance and beyond to the Dada revolution in the arts at the turn of the twentieth century to the experiments in art and technology in the 1960s, collaboration has been an important component of artistic expression.

"CAPTAINS OF INDUSTRY"

As we gradually moved toward our free market economy with individualism as its driving force, however, cooperation and collaboration often were seen as quaint elements of the past. Romantic stories of the great "Captains of

Industry," however, fit nicely with the powerful "great man" narrative that had been developed throughout the years.

REDISCOVERY OF COLLABORATION

In the last century, however, we have begun to "rediscover" the importance of collaboration in virtually every element of our society and economy. Early sociologists such as George Simmel, progressive educators like John Dewey, and, more recently, economic historians such as Evan Rosen have emphasized the growing need for a greater appreciation of collaboration. Each of these individuals and others have sought to reimagine collaboration in our complex, modern world.

DYADS AND TRIADS

George Simmel, often as seen as one of the founders of the field of sociology, introduced the concepts of the dyad (interactions between two individuals) and the triad (three individuals) to illustrate the primary components of cooperation within society. His work provided the intellectual framework for understanding social interaction and has led to a clearer understanding of collaboration in our lives.

EVAN ROSEN

More recently, Evan Rosen has challenged what he calls the "command and control" operations of most business firms today. In a series of books beginning with *The Culture of Collaboration* in 2007, Rosen has given substance to the growing trend in business that is rapidly moving toward collaboration and cooperation rather than the more traditional top-down managerial structure common during the industrial age. Rosen and others have demonstrated that the internet, with its new forms of communication, has accelerated the trend toward collaborative enterprise. We now have begun to recognize that this form of organization promotes both productivity and worker satisfaction. Moreover, as a result of the Pandemic of 2020 and beyond, virtual work has become the norm, demonstrating again the importance of collaboration. Though not a panacea, collaborative enterprise appears to be the future of work.

JOHN DEWEY

In the field of education, John Dewey (chapter 8), was among the first to embrace collaboration and cooperation in the classroom to help students understand the "interconnectedness" of our world. He argued that as the free-market economy became more complex and specialized, we became focused on individualism and lost our connections to one another. For Dewey, the classroom was not only a place for academic learning but also a place to reacquaint students with their important relationships to other people and their occupations.

CONTEMPORARY COLLABORATION IN THE CLASSROOM

Today, new collaborative forms have emerged organically to deal with the growing challenges of diversity in the classroom. Marilyn Friend and Lynne Cooke, in their *Interactions: Collaboration Skills for School Professionals*, for example, have identified six forms of collaboration including parallel teaching, station teaching, and, of course, team teaching. Each form gradually emerged from progressive and neoprogressive ideas as well as teaching professionals in the classrooms.

These few examples illustrate the growing appreciation of collaboration in our world. And by understanding the power of human cooperation, we can then reimagine the development of education. Clearly, the "great men AND women" of the past must be recognized for their contributions to the development of educational ideas, practices, policies, and methods. But we must also place those great men and women in a collaborative context.

As "great" as these individuals may have been, they were the products of collaboration. They stood on the shoulders of others and were fundamentally influenced by their writings. Still others were part of integrated reform groups that developed new ideas through direct conversations and action or were mentored by teachers and professors.

The Arc of Educational Change builds on the basic premise that collaboration is the central element of growth and change. It reassesses education in this context to reimagine its history.

TYPES OF COLLABORATION IN AMERICAN EDUCATIONAL HISTORY

We have identified four general types of collaboration in the history of education. These include intellectual collaboration, movement collaboration, public/private collaboration, and collective impact initiatives. Intellectual collaboration involves the direct exchange of ideas, sometimes through face-to-face networking or careful reading of published works (chapter 1).

With movement collaboration, individuals work together either informally or formally to pursue a reform agenda. This form of collaboration includes efforts to educate the poor (as we will see in chapter 2), to include women in the educational process (chapter 4), and to promote racial and ethnic equity in the classroom (chapter 9).

Public/private collaboration, on the other hand, represents the joint efforts of the state, nongovernmental agencies, and individuals. These partnerships include the work of the Freedmen's Bureau in which the central government marshalled the efforts of reform churches and idealistic schoolteachers to help educate former slave children in the Reconstruction South (chapter 7).

This form of collaboration also was important to the work of mid-nineteenth-century educators to create the common school (chapter 5). Moreover, public/private partnerships were central to the efforts of the founding fathers who embraced different forms of education to support the fragile democracy that they envisioned (chapter 3).

And finally, collective impact initiatives were critical to the intellectual collaboration of philosophers and educators who provided a new foundational structure for education (in chapter 6). The efforts of groups such as the Cincinnati circle that helped to create a more accessible curriculum for the nation's common schools is a good example of this form of collaboration.

Similarly, in chapter 8, we will see how collective impact initiatives were critical to the success of progressive educators in the early twentieth century. And finally, advocates of critical pedagogy today (chapter 10) also reflect this collective impact initiative.

Clearly, there are a number of forms of collaboration, and *The Arc of Educational Change* will address each of them in some detail. In our first chapter, "The Foundationalists," we turn our attention to the key figures of the pre-Enlightenment and Enlightenment eras whose collaboration provided the philosophical and intellectual framework for the development of modern education today.

Chapter 1

The Foundationalists

The intellectual collaboration of individuals we call the foundationalists includes the great empiricists such as Francis Bacon and John Locke, late-Renaissance political theorists like Niccolò Machiavelli and Francesco Guicciardini, and the Enlightenment philosophers Voltaire, Jean-Jacques Rousseau, and Johann Pestalozzi. Understood as a coherent collaborative group, we can better appreciate the emergence of the empirical scientific method, the importance of secular schools, and the need for changes in the discipline of children.

Figure 1.1. Johann Pestalozzi with orphans in Stans. Artist: Konrad Grob, 1879. https://commons.wikimedia.org/wiki/File:Pestalozzi_with_the_orphans_in_Stans.jpg.

FRANCIS BACON

Francis Bacon is considered one of the leading lights of scientific empiricism. Set against an era that was dominated intellectually by the Christian church, he contended that empirical observation and inductive reasoning were the bedrock elements of science. While not rejecting religion, he maintained that observation and reasoning were superior to the "innate ideas" that many church leaders argued had emanated from heaven at birth.

Early Life

Francis Bacon was born in 1561. He was tutored at home during his early years because of his poor health. In fact, his health would be an issue for the great sage throughout his career. At the age of 12 he enrolled at Trinity College, University of Cambridge.

Young Francis drew the attention of a number of important figures during this period, including Dr. John Whitgift, who later would become the Archbishop of Canterbury. Whitgift arranged for young Francis to meet Queen Elizabeth I, who was impressed with Whitgift's protégé. She often referred to Francis as "The Young Lord Keeper," a reference to Bacon's father who was the Lord Keeper of the Great Seal.

Francis continued his education at Cambridge that followed the standard tradition of Latin embedded in the medieval curriculum. It was during this period that he also studied the scientific methods of Aristotle. But while he admired the Greek philosopher a great deal, he gradually began to question Aristotle's basic philosophy.

Career in Law

After his studies at Cambridge, in 1576, Francis and his brother Anthony entered *de societate magistrorum* at Gray's Inn. Here, the young Bacon brothers studied law at one of London's premier institutions. But following the death of his father (Sir Nicholas) in 1579, Francis was left with little income and had to abandon his studies and begin his practice of law as a barrister. Two years later he became a member of parliament, and the following year he was promoted to the position of "outer barrister."

Francis maintained his law practice until 1597 when he attained the prestigious position of Queen's Counsel. Then, when Elizabeth died in 1603, he was knighted by James I and became Baron Bacon Verulam. The following year he married Alice Barnham, a 13-year-old heiress nearly 30 years his junior.

Rise and Fall of His Political Career

Bacon rose quickly in the court of James I and used his skills and influence to mediate disputes between the King and Parliament. Because of these talents, he was eventually elevated to the position of Viscount St. Alban in 1621.

Bacon's meteoric rise to this position of power and authority ended abruptly when he was accused of 23 counts of corruption by his bitter rival, Sir Edward Coke. He was convicted of these charges, fined 40,000 pounds, and spent a few horrifying days in the Tower of London.

Through the intervention of the King, however, his fine was rescinded and he was released from prison. His career as a political figure, however, had come to a rather inglorious end. Nevertheless, this gave Bacon a short but productive period to write, research, and further develop his ideas on scientific empiricism. He would die just five years later in 1626.

Bacon's Criticism of Aristotle

In addition to his successful career as a barrister and a leader in government, Francis Bacon also was a prolific author and scientist. Among his many important philosophical and scientific works, three stand out. The first was *The Proficience and Advancement of Learning*, published in 1605. Then came his masterpiece of intellectual and scientific thought, *Novum Organum*, published in 1620 near the end of his political career. His final work, published posthumously in 1626, was a novel entitled *New Atlantis*.

In his first two works (*The Proficience* and *Novum Organum*), Bacon developed his ideas on empiricism and challenged the prevailing visions of scientific inquiry that had been accepted scientific principles since Aristotle. The great Greek philosopher had presented an alternative to the ideas of Plato regarding the scientific method. In a classic statement on this subject, Aristotle had written that "to gain light on things imperceptible, we must use the evidence of perceptible things."

While Bacon greatly admired Aristotle and generally embraced many of his concepts, he argued that his ideas were incomplete in three fundamental ways. First, he rejected Aristotle's use of deductive reasoning to understand phenomena in nature. Second, Bacon was troubled that the great scholar was still wedded to religion in his understanding of philosophy and logic. And finally, he challenged Aristotle's idea that the mind was a "blank slate" at birth.

Deduction versus Induction

Aristotle began his understanding of phenomena through a deductive process. By starting with innate ideas embedded in philosophy and theology, he then collected information to understand the laws of nature. Bacon rejected this approach and essentially turned this process on its head by calling for inductive reasoning.

In his *Novum Organum*, Bacon argued that we begin scientific inquiry with specific information that we observe empirically, and then use these facts and data to build theory. In short, while Aristotle developed his ideas by arguing from the general to the specific, Bacon did so by beginning with the specific and moving to the general.

A Challenge to Religion

Bacon also rejected Aristotle's reliance on religion to understand natural phenomena. In his *Novum Organum* he wrote that the idea of mixing science with "superstition and theology [was] most injurious to it both as a whole and in parts."

Then, in *The Proficience*, Bacon proposed his "famous distempers of Learning," which included the three types of unproductive learning: the fantastical, the contentious, and the delicate. Each of these, he argued, were pursued by linking religion to scientific analysis.

Rejection of the Blank Slate

Finally, Bacon criticized the general idea of the mind as a blank slate. Rather, he argued that the mind was "like an enchanted glass full of superstition and imposture." These "idols," as he called them, had to be faced and eliminated before empirical study could begin. In short, Bacon argued that our own personal biases (which he summarized as the four idols: the tribe, the cave, the marketplace, and the theater) could interfere with rigorous empirical analysis.

New Atlantis

In his final work, *New Atlantis*, Bacon applied many of these new ideas in a more accessible format. This novel dealt with a futuristic community of scholars who used empirical methods to make new discoveries and improve society. This utopian world envisioned by Bacon was one where "generosity and enlightenment . . . (as well as) public spirit were the essential qualities of this land."

Bacon passed from the earth in 1626 of pneumonia while conducting his final scientific experiment. He had observed empirically that meat could be preserved by placing it in a cold environment, and set out to prove his hypothesis, based on his own observations. Bacon had a chicken prepared, placed it in the snow, and monitored the process. Before long, however, he was overcome by the cold and was brought to the home of a friend, the Earl of Arundel, who lived nearby. Francis Bacon died shortly thereafter.

Scientific Legacy

Bacon's death ended a long and illustrious career in law and in politics. More importantly, however, he laid the philosophical foundation of the scientific method by embracing empiricism and the inductive process of reasoning. He also called for the clear separation of scientific inquiry and religious belief, and recognized the inherent biases in the human mind. As such, he helped to launch the scientific revolution of the 1600s and collaborated intellectually with other scholars to break from the constraints of theology.

RENAISSANCE SCHOLARS

Paralleling the work of Bacon were the late Italian Renaissance scholars such as Niccolò Machiavelli, Francesco Guicciardini, and Bernardino Telesio. These political theorists began to question the narrowly focused, religiously oriented vision of knowledge presented by the Catholic Church.

Machiavelli challenged the basis of sovereignty and political leadership by arguing that rulers were not endowed with the right to rule by God but, through a kind of "realpolitik," they maintained their power. Here, the divine spiritual basis of royal authority was rejected in favor of a direct observation of how these rulers gained their power and maintained it. Like future scholars, Machiavelli used empirical methods to understand politics.

Guicciardini, on the other hand, used modern historical techniques, including the analysis of primary documents, to understand Italian history. His works *The History of Florence* and *The History of Italy* were both rooted in this modern empirical approach. He noted that all the actions of political rulers were motivated by their own self-interest rather than divine intervention.

Bernardino Telesio was an important link between the Renaissance scholars of this era and the English empiricists Francis Bacon and John Locke. Telesio was a central figure or contemporary of these towering figures in the late Renaissance intellectual movement against what was called abstract reason.

Like others in his circle, Telesio argued that knowledge could not be derived by reason alone but must "be understood by means of observation."

This reliance on empirical observation led Bacon to call Telesio the "first of the moderns."

INTELLECTUAL COLLABORATION

Thus, when Francis Bacon began to develop his ideas of empirical analysis, he had an intellectual collaboration with Aristotle. But he also influenced the growing literature of Renaissance scholars who embraced empirical observation as the basis of knowledge.

JOHN LOCKE

While Francis Bacon was an early advocate of empiricism, John Locke developed these ideas further. Locke was born on August 29, 1632, just four years after the death of Bacon. Both of his parents were strict Puritans, and his father was a captain in the cavalry of the Parliamentarians in the English Civil War. When he was just 15 years old, Locke was sent to study at the Westminster school and, at the age of 20, was admitted to Christ Church, Oxford.

Early Life and Education

Although Locke was a decent student, he was critical of the undergraduate curriculum that was still mired in the medieval classical tradition. Rather, he was more interested in modern philosophers. At Oxford he also became fascinated with medicine. Nevertheless, he continued his undergraduate studies and earned his bachelor's degree in 1656 and his master of arts in 1658. He would later receive his bachelor of medicine degree in 1675.

Locke Gains Notoriety

It was in the field of medicine that John Locke made an early name for himself when serving as Lord Ashley's personal physician. When Ashley suffered a near-fatal bout of liver failure due to a large cyst embedded in the organ, Locke successfully operated on him and saved his life.

Lord Ashley, one of the key Whig figures of this period, took John under his wing and had a profound impact on the young man. While Ashley became Lord Chancellor in 1672, Locke became tangentially involved in politics himself. And yet, his political career stalled when Ashley's meteoric rise was temporarily detoured. Locke then traveled to France, where he further developed his skills as a physician.

Major Works

Throughout this period, however, Locke maintained his interest in politics and philosophy. When he returned to England, he began his influential *Two Treatises of Government*. These works fundamentally challenged absolute monarchy and promoted the idea of the natural rights of man.

But just as his scientific career had begun to blossom, Locke was implicated in the so-called Rye House Plot against the government, and was forced into exile in Amsterdam. It was there that he was influenced by the freethinkers of the Spinoza circle and further developed his ideas on political and religious tolerance as well as the separation of church and state.

During this crucial period, John had the time, energy, and intellectual stimulation to continue his *Two Treatises of Government*, *An Essay Concerning Human Understanding*, and his *Letter Concerning Toleration*. When he returned to London in the aftermath of the Glorious Revolution in January 1689, he was able to finish these three important works, all of which were published within a year of his return.

Whig Movement

For the next decade, until his death in 1704, Locke became a major figure in the Whig movement. As the opposition party to the conservative Tories, Whigs challenged absolute monarchy. Instead they favored a representative form of government as well as a more open, free market economic system. These pillars would define modern liberalism.

Locke's Intellectual Contributions

John Locke's intellectual achievements cannot be overstated. His political theory and practice, as well as his direct contributions to the development of modern education, were monumental. Locke clearly was influenced by Bacon's inductive reasoning and his rejection of "innate knowledge." Indeed, as Locke argued, all knowledge was gained through experience and education.

In addition, John Locke is considered the father of liberalism with his *Two Treatises on Government*. Enlightenment figures such as Voltaire, for example, were influenced by Locke's writings. In fact, Voltaire once referred to him as "le sage Locke."

Later, Jefferson, Madison, Hamilton, and other "Founding Fathers" of the American Revolution carefully read Locke and were greatly influenced by "the sage." Locke's *Two Treatises of Government* (especially his second treatise) were studied by most of the leaders of the American Revolution.

His emphasis on the natural rights of man and contract theory clearly were embedded in both the Declaration of Independence and more forcefully in the U.S. Constitution.

Locke also had argued that individual rights of man were "inalienable" and could not be taken or given away. For him, natural rights were "life, liberty, and property." Moreover, his ideas regarding "social contract theory" were equally as important, and he argued that they represent the "glue" that holds society together. In its simplest terms, contract theory supports the idea that individuals in society give up some of their freedom and submit to a legal authority to protect their basic freedoms and maintain a free society.

Locke and Education

Beyond these important political and philosophical contributions, however, Locke also had a profound influence on educators for more than three centuries. His recognition of the importance of education as the only path to progress, his call for the separation of religion and education, and his rejection of the inhumane discipline of children derived from biblical imperatives, all have impacted the development of modern educational thought throughout the years.

Major Educational Writings

John Locke's *An Essay Concerning Human Understanding* (1690) and *Some Thoughts Concerning Education*, published in 1693, provided a new perspective on education. His "theory of the mind," for example, embedded in *An Essay Concerning Human Understanding*, argued that children were born as blank slates and that only through education could they develop and learn. Clearly, Locke embraced empiricism as the basis of education.

Locke's second major work on education was *Some Thoughts Concerning Education*. While *Human Understanding* was more philosophical in nature, *Some Thoughts* focused on the practical elements of education. For Locke, education had three distinct components: developing a healthy body, forming a virtuous character, and selecting an appropriate curriculum for the child.

Discipline

As part of his ideas on developing a healthy body, Locke rejected the brutal physical punishment of children in both schools and at home. The biblical concept of "original sin" held that children were "stained" at birth, and that only through severe physical discipline could they be saved from the influences of the devil.

Biblical imperatives, such as "Spare the rod and spoil the child," appear in Proverbs 13:24 and then six additional times in this book alone. For example, Proverbs 23:14 states: "Thou shalt beat him with the rod and shalt deliver his soul from hell." Similarly, Proverbs 22:15 states: "Foolishness is bound in the heart of a child, but the rod of correction shall drive it from him."

These biblical directives gave credibility to corporal punishment and, even as late as the 1500s, most pedagogues agreed that it was appropriate to whip children to discipline them. In fact, Richard Mulcaster, famed teacher and tutor to Princess Elizabeth of England, once wrote that the "rod may no more be spared in schools than the sword may in the prince's hand."

By the late 1600s and early 1700s, Locke's ideas began to have an effect not only on the separation of religion from the curriculum of schools, but also on the age-old idea that children must be beaten because of the stain of original sin. For Locke, corporal punishment was the most egregious form of correction. Rather, he favored a disciplinary approach that included praise for good behavior matched with humiliation for misbehavior. A new era of discipline was now slowly emerging.

THE FRENCH ENLIGHTENMENT

The intellectual collaboration of the early English empiricists Francis Bacon and John Locke had a critical influence on the French Enlightenment philosophers, especially Voltaire, Jean-Jacques Rousseau, and Johann Pestalozzi from nearby Switzerland.

VOLTAIRE

During the mid- to late 1700s, Voltaire was a dominant figure in French philosophy, history, and literature. Profoundly influenced by Francis Bacon, Voltaire was a fierce advocate of empiricism as a pathway to understanding both past and present society. Voltaire also was a strong advocate of freedom of speech and the total separation of church and state.

Voltaire, baptized Francois-Marie Arouet, was born in November 1694 in Paris. His father, Francois Arouet, was a lawyer and worked for the French government. His mother, Marie Marguerite Daumard, came from a minor noble family.

Voltaire received a classical religious education from the Jesuits, and he studied Latin, theology, and rhetoric. Later he learned modern languages and became fluent in Italian, Spanish, and English.

Father's Influence

Voltaire wanted to pursue a career as a writer, but his father insisted that he become a lawyer. Voltaire went through the motions of working as an assistant to a notary in Paris, but secretly wrote poetry. Soon, however, his father discovered the ruse and sent the young boy to Caen in Normandy to study law.

Nevertheless, Voltaire continued his writing and, because of his talent and wit, he became the darling of aristocrats in and around Normandy. His studies suffered. But his father was determined to direct his son's career toward the law and arranged for Voltaire to become secretary to the French ambassador to the Netherlands.

This position, however, was short-lived. Voltaire's love affair with a young French refugee caused a major scandal at The Hague and he was sent back to Paris. Meanwhile, his growing political consciousness landed him in serious trouble. In one of his essays, he accused the regent (the Duke of Orleans) of incest with his daughter and, as a result, he was imprisoned in the Bastille for nearly a year.

Success as a Writer

Following his release, Voltaire continued to write and soon became quite successful. His *Edipe* had a long run at the Comédie-Française and was such a success that Voltaire was awarded a distinguished medal by King George in 1718. Shortly thereafter the French regent (perhaps reluctantly) presented him with another medal of appreciation. Voltaire was just 24 years old!

During the next few years, Voltaire had mixed success with his writing. Two of his plays were failures, but his epic 1722 poem *La Henriade* about Henry IV of France was a major success. The poem caught the attention of Lord Bolingbroke, and Voltaire developed a long friendship with the exiled radical English Jacobite.

Voltaire's Political Transformation

In fact, Voltaire's transformation from a successful man of letters who wrote poems, plays, and satires to a more serious philosopher came in the early 1720s during his stay with the exiled Lord Bolingbroke at his estate near Orleans, France.

It was here that Voltaire was introduced to the British empiricism of Francis Bacon and John Locke as well as the ideas of natural philosophy. Voltaire also collaborated with the freethinkers in the Bolingbroke circle.

These intellectuals prided themselves on independent free thinking and often rejected all religious teachings.

The contacts that Voltaire made here profoundly influenced his ideas on formalized religion, religious freedom, and diversity and his embrace of secularism. These ideas have now become the solid bedrock of modern educational thought.

A few years after his return to Paris from Orleans, Voltaire had a verbal argument with Chevalier de Rohan. In retaliation, de Rohan hired henchmen to beat up Voltaire. When Voltaire recovered from his beating, he challenged Chevalier to a duel, but the powerful de Rohan family instead arranged to have Voltaire imprisoned in the Bastille.

Exile to England

Fearing a life behind bars, Voltaire was able to negotiate his exile to England as an alternative to prison. He was granted this request, and his intellectual life would be changed forever. In England Voltaire renewed his friendship with Bolingbroke, who had returned to England in 1723. Here he also met and collaborated with Jonathan Swift, Alexander Pope, and John Gay and interacted with members of high society.

Voltaire's experience in England had a major impact on him. He began to recognize that English constitutionalism was a superior system of government compared to the despotism of the French monarchy. Moreover, he admired the greater freedom of speech and religion in England as compared to France. Voltaire was also influenced by the literature, poetry, and satirical writing of Swift and Pope and was inspired by the work of Gay and, of course, the plays and sonnets of Shakespeare.

Voltaire returned to France in 1729 a different person, with a different outlook on life. Lord Morley, one of his closest patrons, once commented that Voltaire "left France as a poet and returned as its sage."

Letters on the English

Voltaire did not immediately return to Paris. He spent several months in a small fishing port in Normandy until he finally was allowed to return to the City of Lights. During the next few months, Voltaire made some successful investments and had a little luck on the lottery. As a result, he became financially independent for the first time in his life. As usual, however, trouble would follow. But this time it was "good trouble."

In 1733, Voltaire published *Lettres philosophiques* (*Letters on the English*) that praised the British constitutional monarchy. He wrote that the British were more accepting of human rights and religious tolerance than were the French.

Newton versus Descartes

In addition, his *Letters* immersed Voltaire in the raging controversy over Newtonianism. Voltaire championed the English Newton over the French Descartes and used this as the basic framework to compare the philosophical tradition of scientific empiricism with the religious-based Cartesian (Descartes) philosophy. In doing so, Voltaire placed himself firmly among the younger members of the Royal Academy of Science in Paris and against the established members of this body. This caused a major scandal; Voltaire's books were burned, and he was forced into exile once again.

Émilie du Châtelet: Intellectual Partner

This time he fled to the Champagne region of France and began an affair with the lovely mathematician Émilie du Châtelet. Du Châtelet became his intellectual partner and muse for more than a decade.

Voltaire's relationship with this intelligent and scholarly woman both enhanced his general philosophical and scientific development and gave him an appreciation of women's rights. It was at her husband's *Cirey* chateau that Voltaire amassed a great library, studied history, and performed scientific experiments based on Newtonian concepts with his intellectual partner, Émilie.

Together, Voltaire and du Châtelet promoted the ideas of Newtonian science and often referred to the old guard French science as "backward Cartesianism." For her part, du Châtelet wrote a favorable review of Voltaire's position in the *Journal des Savants* and both she and Voltaire received honorable mentions in 1739 from the Paris Academy for their work on the nature of fire.

Most scholars today agree that their steadfast support of Newtonian science, embedded in the empiricism of Bacon and Locke, helped to convert the French scientific community to Newtonianism from Cartesianism by the 1750s.

Prussia and Exile to Switzerland

When du Châtelet died during childbirth in 1749, a heartbroken Voltaire left France and traveled to Prussia. Here he was greeted with honors by Frederick the Great and his court. But after a little more than a year, Voltaire's satirical writings led to trouble once again. In 1752, he left Berlin in a flurry of scandal, but rather than returning to France, he settled in Geneva. And yet here, too, he was not welcome.

Voltaire's Legacy

Frustrated with public intellectual life, Voltaire purchased a country chateau at Ferney. He remained there for the next two decades until his return to France in 1778. By then, his reputation had grown and he was considered the "hero of the Enlightenment." He returned to Paris as a major celebrity to attend the opening of his final play, *Irène*, and died just weeks later.

Religious Tolerance

Voltaire was a deist. He believed in what he called "an external, supreme and intelligent being" but challenged formalized religion and its powerful hold over French society, politics, and education. Nevertheless, Voltaire also believed in religious and ethnic tolerance. Not only did he argue that all sects of Christianity should tolerate one another, but that we should "regard all men as our brothers." These included the "Turks, the Chinaman, the Jew and the Siam."

While critical of most formal religions, Voltaire praised Hindus for embracing a philosophy that he felt was both peaceful and "innocent." Hindus, he wrote, were "incapable of hurting others or of defending themselves." Moreover, their cultural acceptance of vegetarianism led Voltaire to become a vegetarian himself. He also believed strongly in animal rights.

Voltaire's progressive ideas provided a foundation for modern schools that were secular in nature, and critical of the overarching power of priests, ministers, and organized religion in general. His stance on tolerance, diversity, and women's rights, moreover, stand as important pillars of modern education.

JEAN-JACQUES ROUSSEAU

While many enlightenment scholars were influenced by Bacon's empiricism and the revolutionary ideas of John Locke, Jean-Jacques Rousseau played a central role in promoting these modern educational ideas.

Early Life

Jean-Jacques Rousseau was born in Geneva on June 28, 1712, eight years after the death of John Locke. His mother died nine days after his birth, and he was raised by his father and aunt. He lived his first few years in a wealthier section of the city, but because of some financial difficulties, the family was forced to sell their home and move to an artisan neighborhood. It was here that Rousseau developed his understanding of class and his appreciation of the work of artisans and other skilled workers.

Rousseau's father encouraged the young boy to read, and by the age of five or six Jean-Jacques and his father were routinely reading adventure stories to one another. Rousseau later wrote that the two would read all night and "sometimes in the morning on hearing the swallows at our window," his exhausted father would beg his son to come to bed. Later he and his father continued their reading of Plutarch and other classical scholars.

At the age of ten, Jean Jacque's father remarried, and the young boy was sent to live with his uncle and then, in turn, was enrolled in a boarding school run by a Calvinist minister. It was here that Jean-Jacques studied mathematics and drawing.

His early education ended abruptly, however, when he was sent out to an engraver as an apprentice. The engraver regularly beat the young boy. Rousseau endured this treatment for more than a year, but then he ran away to Geneva. As the story goes, when he entered the city one evening, he found that the gates were locked because of a curfew.

Françoise-Louise de Warens

Rousseau then sought the help of a Roman Catholic priest who in turn introduced him to Françoise-Louise de Warens, a Protestant noblewoman more than ten years his senior. Through her patronage, Rousseau was able to continue his education and had many interesting life experiences.

When Rousseau turned 20, the two became lovers, and he was also introduced to de Warens's inner circle. For the next several years he pursued his studies, read from de Warens's extensive library, and interacted with a group of intellectual elites. It was during this period, moreover, that he developed an early interest in philosophy.

Return to Paris

In his mid-20s, Rousseau received a small inheritance and with it repaid his debt to de Warens and set out on his own. He moved to France and took a position as a tutor to a wealthy family in Lyon.

During the next few years, he developed a system of musical notation, and, in 1742, Rousseau moved to Paris, where he presented his method to the Académie des Sciences. While his new system was rejected by the Académie, he did receive some positive comments and encouragement to continue his work. Disappointed, he did not.

Rousseau then accepted a post as secretary to the Comte de Montague, the French ambassador to Venice. Although he gained a great deal of experience, he was not paid well and after just a year in the post he resigned and returned to Paris, penniless.

Soon thereafter, Rousseau met Thérèse Levasseur. Once he was on his feet financially, he brought Thérèse, her mother, and several siblings into his household and supported them. There is some evidence, especially from Rousseau's *Confessions*, that Levasseur bore him at least four children, each of whom was sent to a "foundling hospital." While she was not happy with this decision, both her mother and Rousseau had pressured her to do so to protect her "honor."

Fame and Criticism

Later, when Rousseau gained considerable fame with the publication of *Emile*, his education novel, a number of enlightenment figures including Voltaire criticized him for his seeming disregard for his own children. In his *Confessions*, however, Rousseau claimed that his actions were in the best interests of his children's education.

Meanwhile, Rousseau continued to write, and by the end of the 1740s had published a number of articles on music and contributed several pieces to the *Encyclopedia* of Diderot and D'Alembert. Then, in 1755, he published his influential article *A Discourse on Political Economy*, from which he gained considerable recognition.

The next few years were rather tumultuous for Rousseau. His affair with Sophie d'Houdetot who was a houseguest of Rousseau's patron, Madame d'Épinay, caused considerable friction. This led to insults and eventually a break from a group of Encyclopedists (including Diderot) who were part of d'Épinay's circle. Still bitter from this incident, Diderot later referred to Jean Jacques as "false, vain as Satan, ungrateful, cruel, hypocritical and wicked."

But Rousseau would have the last word. His publication in 1761 of *Julie*, a novel that was based on his relationship with Sophie, was an enormous success and ultimately secured Rousseau's financial position.

Two Educational Works

In the spring of the following year, however, Rousseau penned two important works that were to revolutionize both the concepts of government and education. It was these two works that established him as an intellectual force and secured his reputation in promoting modern educational ideas.

The Social Contract

The Social Contract, published in April 1762, was an important blueprint for nations dealing with the growing problem of creating and maintaining an interdependent society in the face of the growing individualism associated with the free market economy. His classic statement that began this work, however, became a mantra for generations of educators. Rousseau wrote, "Man is born free and everywhere he is in chains."

For Rousseau, traditional society and government had restricted human freedom and, as a result, had created inequality. Man was born free and pure—it was society itself that diminished that freedom. Given this idea, educators gradually embraced new attitudes toward the discipline of children. Rather than perceiving them as wicked and evil, in need of physical punishment to "change their evil ways," more humane approaches were slowly developed.

Emile

The following month, Rousseau's classic work on education was published. Titled *Emile or On Education*, this novel applied many of the ideas he had developed in *The Social Contract*. By focusing on Emile from an early age through his maturity, marriage, and career, however, Rousseau was able to demonstrate what he saw as a new and appropriate form of education. The goal of education, as he saw it, was to help children become well-balanced, open-minded individuals in a natural setting without the restrictions and burdens imposed by society.

JOHANN HEINRICH PESTALOZZI

With the exception of Rousseau's masterful educational novel, *Emile*, educational foundationalists typically centered their attention on both the philosophical and scientific elements on which modern education would be built. This however, was not the case with Johann Heinrich Pestalozzi. Pestalozzi (1746–1827) was an educator, teacher, and writer who applied the ideas of other educational philosophers to the classroom.

Pestalozzi's two classic novels, *Leonard and Gertrude* (1781) and *How Gertrude Teaches Her Children* (1801), brought the somewhat abstract ideas of child-centered learning to life. In these works, Pestalozzi introduced us to Gertrude—the loving teacher who used everyday items to teach her children. It was Gertrude's love and her innovative teaching methods that defined the modern child-centered approach to education.

In *Leonard and Gertrude*, Pestalozzi demonstrates how Gertrude taught arithmetic. She had her students count "the number of steps from one end of the room to the other." They also counted the "threads while spinning and the number of turns on the reel when they wound the yarn onto skeins."
How Gertrude Teaches Her Children, on the other hand, focused on how the love of a mother and, later, of the teacher helped to develop the consciousness of the child. Pestalozzi wrote that the "first instruction of the child [should be the] business of the senses." Only when the senses of the child have been developed could education move to the realm of reason.

As a young man Pestalozzi worked in relative obscurity, though his ideas were spreading throughout Europe. In 1805, however, this changed. That year John Griscom, a social reformer, traveled to Switzerland to observe Pestalozzi in the classroom. Griscom was fascinated with Pestalozzi, and, in 1808, he published his *A Year in Europe*, which described in detail the success of Pestalozzi's methods.

Griscom wrote that Pestalozzi's class of 90 boys was instructed by one teacher with no books. Nevertheless, the teacher was "constantly with a child, always talking, questioning, explaining and repeating." Griscom praised what he called the "moral charm of this method," noting that it was superior to other forms of instruction.

Within a decade, Pestalozzi's ideas were being adopted in England and the United States. Charles Mayo and his sister Elizabeth Mayo, for example, were profoundly influenced by Pestalozzi. The Mayos established a number of "infant schools" in England based on Pestalozzi's methods, while Elizabeth helped establish the first "infant schools" teacher training schools.

In Germany, Friedrich Froebel, a student of Pestalozzi, developed the idea of the "kindergarten" and established dozens of these schools throughout Prussia. But the so-called *kindergarten-verbot* edit of 1851 referred to his schools as "atheistic and demagogic [with] destructive tendencies in the areas of religion and politics."

While the edict was based on a confusion with Froebel's nephew, who had criticized the Prussian government, the effect on the kindergarten movement was devastating and led to a virtual diaspora of German kindergarten teachers.

Ironically, one of the dispersed teachers, Margaret Schurz, fled to the United States and established a German-speaking kindergarten in Watertown, Wisconsin, in 1856. Later, Elizabeth Peabody (sister of Mary Tyler Peabody Mann, the wife of Horace Mann) was influenced by Schurz and established her own kindergarten in Boston in 1860.

Clearly, Pestalozzi's influence was powerful and widespread. He adopted many of the ideas of the early foundationalists, and through his educational novels and personal work in the classroom, he spread the ideas of child-centered learning throughout Europe and the United States. Derived from his intellectual collaboration with Locke, Rousseau, Voltaire, and others, Pestalozzi promoted a new vision of education that was embraced by hundreds of other child-centered educators.

INTELLECTUAL COLLABORATION

The intellectual collaboration among these important figures was complex. We began our discussion with Francis Bacon and his important contributions using both inductive reasoning and empirical observation of phenomena. As we have seen, these became the cornerstones of modern scientific inquiry.

Late Italian Renaissance scholars expanded these ideas into the realm of politics, philosophy, and history. Machiavelli articulated a powerful reassessment of the basis of political power and flatly rejected the "divine right of Kings" as the basis of their authority. Rather, it was a function of "realpolitik," raw political power stripped from its religious foundation.

Guicciardini carried on this tradition in the field of history by empirically examining primary documents to understand the past. Finally, Telesio's vigorous embrace of empirical analysis led Bacon to refer to him as "the first of the moderns."

In short, Francis Bacon stood on the shoulders of the great Greek philosophers and contemporary Renaissance scholars to develop a modern form of scientific empiricism that employed inductive reasoning and careful observation. His intellectual collaboration was deep and broad.

John Locke, of course, was influenced not only by the ancients but by Bacon himself. His vision of empirical science was well developed, and he expanded both political and educational ideas that would transform western society. Locke understood well that the modern empirical approach was not confined to scientific discovery but was central to political theory, philosophy, and education.

Locke's political ideas of the inalienable rights of man provided a basis for both Enlightenment philosophers as well as the Founding Fathers of the American Revolution and constitutional period. His social contract theory held that a fundamental agreement between society and individuals was necessary to maintain a complex modern world.

Locke's philosophical approach also inspired a generation of political leaders and activists in the French Enlightenment, and his application of modern scientific methods to knowledge demanded a new approach to education. Here, he argued for a separation of religion and education, a proper curriculum suitable for students at different ages, and one that emphasized the importance of physical development as well as mental acuity. And finally

Locke favored a new disciplinary approach to children that rejected corporal punishment.

The French Enlightenment figures of Voltaire, Rousseau, and Pestalozzi, as well as a handful of others, also were dramatically influenced by Bacon's empiricism and Locke's ideas of separation of church and state. Voltaire, perhaps the central figure in the French Enlightenment, had traveled to England and lived there for years and was profoundly moved by Locke's approach to religion. He rejected the powerful influence of formal religion in society, politics, and education, but nevertheless argued for religious toleration and diversity.

Regarding political theory, Voltaire favored the constitutionalism of England over the despotism of French monarchy. And finally, his vision of scientific empiricism was rooted in Newtonianism rejecting the prevailing Cartesian (Decartes) philosophy that dominated French intellectual thought during the first half of the eighteenth century.

The collaborative link between Voltaire and his younger colleague, Jean-Jacques Rousseau, was rooted in Voltaire's' *Letteres philosophiques* that celebrated both human rights and religious tolerance. Rousseau was influenced by these ideas along with the educational writings of John Locke as the basis of both his *Social Contract* and his masterwork of education, *Emile*.

Finally, it was the work of Pestalozzi that brought many of these ideas to fruition. His practical application of the foundationalists' vision, his extraordinary work in the classroom, and his educational novels together promoted a new course for child-centered education.

Clearly, the foundationalists—from the empiricists Francis Bacon and John Locke to the great philosophers of the Enlightenment including Voltaire and Rousseau, to the application of these ideas by Pestalozzi, helped to transform education. By emphasizing the importance of inductive reasoning, establishing the basis of the scientific method, demanding a separation of church, state, and education, recognizing the impediments of society on the development of children, and challenging the biblical traditions of severe corporal punishment, the foundationalists helped to establish an educational renaissance.

Chapter 2

Advocates for the Poor

The foundationalists provided us with a rich source of progressive, child-centered ideas that would transform our collective vision of education. One of the earliest expressions of this was the work of the advocates of the poor. The central role of the early Quakers, their work with the emancipation and education of enslaved African Americans, as well as their influence on Joseph Lancaster and his efforts to educate the poor, opened the door to a more inclusive and universal educational system.

While the collaborative form of the foundationalists was primarily intellectual—achieved through the sharing of ideas and publications—such Quakers as John Woolman, George Fox, Thomas Budd, William Penn, and later Joseph Lancaster collaborated with a shared sense of humanitarianism developed through religion.

Figure 2.1. Lancaster School opened in 1809. Photo by Tony Hisgett, 2010. https://commons.wikimedia.org/wiki/File:British_School_(4967589423).jpg.

WILLIAM PENN

In the American colonies, the movement toward both abolition of slavery and the education of African American children was promoted by a number of Quaker philanthropists, including William Penn. Penn provided a critical link between the growing Quaker movement collaboration in England and the American colonies.

Penn was awarded an enormous tract of land in what is now Pennsylvania as payment of the King's debt to his father, Sir William Penn. Penn established the colony with the intention of guaranteeing religious tolerance and extending manhood suffrage for settlers of all faiths.

His strong beliefs, articulated in his "Great Law" or "Frame of Government" in 1682, reflected his defense of pacificism, equality, humanitarianism, and education. These provisions would not only strengthen the foundation of the movement in the colonies, but they also provided a new perspective on the less fortunate.

Through Penn's influence, the Pennsylvania Friends established a school in 1689 that served not only the rich, but also the poor. This was an extension of the Quaker tradition of education for orphans and the poor through subscription schools.

Penn's humanitarianism also had an impact on the early abolitionist movement both in England and in the colonies. For example, in 1688, a number of Quakers from Germantown, Pennsylvania, issued a protest against slavery and began a long and vigorous debate among Quakers concerning the morality of slavery.

JOHN WOOLMAN: ABOLITIONIST AND EDUCATOR

It was this new humanitarian sensibility that appealed to many young Quakers in the early- to mid-eighteenth century. Among these new Quaker abolitionists was John Woolman. As a young man Woolman was influenced by the growing abolitionist movement within the English Quaker community. He spent much of his early life as a traveling minister and vigorously promoted the cause of abolition.

In 1754, he wrote a powerful abolitionist pamphlet titled "Some Considerations on the keeping of Negroes." This placed Woolman at the forefront of the new abolitionist crusade, and it appears that a young Joseph Lancaster also was profoundly influenced by his sentiments. As we will see, young Lancaster was so moved by the plight of enslaved Africans in the Caribbean that he packed his bags and set off to "teach the slaves."

Woolman not only argued for the end to slavery but also the education of enslaved Africans. He challenged members of the Friends community to provide a Christian education for these unfortunate people. He wrote that it was the responsibility of the Friends to provide "a Christian education and a suitable opportunity for improving the mind." Woolman concluded by writing "for the way of life of one is made grievous by the rigor of another, it entails misery to both."

ANTHONY BENEZET

Another important new abolitionist of the early- to mid-eighteenth century was Anthony Benezet, a close friend and collaborator of John Woolman. Benezet, originally a French Huguenot, was drawn to the ideas of the Quakers and officially converted in 1726, when he was just 14 years old.

Later, in 1731, he migrated with his family to Pennsylvania, where he met and joined John Woolman to become a "radical" abolitionist. Soon he began teaching in Germantown, Pennsylvania, and later he taught in Philadelphia's English Friends School.

True to his humanitarian abolitionism, Benezet also taught enslaved Africans at night. Several years later, he opened a private "girls' school" funded from his own meager salary. Then later in life, Benezet founded the Negro School of Philadelphia that supported the growing free black community in the "City of Brotherly Love."

Throughout his career as a teacher, Benezet continued his advocacy for abolition. In 1775, he helped to establish the first anti-slavery society in the American colonies—the Society for the Relief of Free Negroes Unlawfully Held in Bondage. Following Benezet's death, the "Society" was reorganized as the Pennsylvania Abolitionist Society.

QUAKERS AND THEIR LEGACY

Interestingly, Benjamin Franklin became the president of this organization and was persuaded to bring the issue of abolition to the Constitutional Convention in 1787. Franklin did so but unfortunately, it never made it into the U.S. Constitution because of opposition from Southern delegates. Franklin tried again to ban slavery in the United States in 1790, but the measure was defeated.

The work of Quakers George Fox, John Woolman, and Anthony Benezet on both sides of the Atlantic illustrate not only the struggle for abolition and education for enslaved and free blacks, but also provides a link to the important work of Joseph Lancaster and his quest to educate the "new poor."

The intellectual and movement collaboration of the early Quaker abolitionists and Joseph Lancaster had a profound impact on the overall development of new educational ideas, especially in the area of universal education.

JOSEPH LANCASTER: YOUTHFUL ENTHUSIASM

Joseph Lancaster was born in 1778 to a middle-class family in Southwark, England, just outside of London. Not much is known of his early life, but it appears he had religious visions as a child that directed him to teach poor blacks the word of God. Then at the age of 14, he read an article documenting the horrific lives of enslaved Africans in Jamaica and he was moved to action.

Young Joseph packed his bag and made his way to the port of Bristol, an arduous journey of about 100 miles. When he finally arrived in the bustling port city, however, he found he did not have enough money for the trip to the West Indies. To survive, he took a number of odd jobs in Bristol and soon met a group of Quakers who encouraged him to join the Society of Friends.

Joseph was a spiritually oriented and deeply religious young man, but he had rejected his family's pressure to become a minister. Nevertheless, he was fascinated with the Quakers' simple lifestyle, activist orientation, and embrace of equality (especially abolitionism). His on-and-off collaboration with members of the Society of Friends would guide him throughout his life.

Teaching the Poor

While young Joseph did not get to the West Indies, his desire to right the wrongs of society and provide a useful service to his new religion remained strong. Within just a few years of his conversion, while still in his teens, young Joseph turned his attention to another unfortunate group—the sons and daughters of the working poor of London.

These children of the "new working class" had little chance for survival and faced a bleak future. Many reform-minded men and women during this period were appalled by the condition of the new poor, especially the children, but unlike other reformers, Lancaster acted.

Borough Road School

At the age of 20, Lancaster opened his first school in his father's home. Outside his new school he placed as sign that read: "All those who will may send their children and have them educated freely, and those who do not wish to have education for nothing, may pay for it if they please." His enrollment at the school grew dramatically and soon he was forced to find another building that would accommodate nearly 200 children. With the support of several Quaker benefactors, he found a suitable building and on January 1, 1798, he opened his famous Borough Road School.

Joseph Lancaster's work in education was the product of a reform-minded movement collaboration. His humanitarianism emerged from his powerful connection to the Friends, their work as abolitionists within that community, and their early efforts to establish schools for the poor, both black and white.

The Monitorial System

While Lancaster was an idealistic Quaker humanitarian, he also was a pragmatist. Lancaster understood that with neither tuition from his students nor consistent funding from his benefactors, his school would fail. As a result, he developed a new form of teaching known as the monitorial system that employed older, more advanced students to teach groups of younger students.

His system was similar to Andrew Bell's Madras schools that were developed about the same time in India. But while Bell's schools typically were designed for small groups of children in charity orphanages and were supported financially by the Church of England, Lancaster's schools were much larger, non-sectarian, and intended for the children of the working poor.

Lancaster's system was both ingenious and successful. Although criticized by many, he helped establish his monitorial schools throughout England, Europe, the United States, Mexico, and in several South American nations.

Market-Based System

Lancaster understood that the new market economy that was emerging in both England and the United Sates had created major divisions between the "haves" and the "have nots." But rather than challenging this powerful economy, he embraced many of its concepts and incorporated them into his new school.

In fact, as educational historian David Hogan has noted, his system "was based on individual competition, a meritocratic structure, and a classroom psychology (of) scarcity, desire, ambition, shame and humiliation." Moreover, despite his deeply held religious convictions, the "controlling concepts and metaphors (of his schools) were commercial and disciplinary, not religious."

Lancaster's Quaker humanism, linked to his pragmatic approach to education, opened the door to the modern schools of today. His contributions to education were enormous. He was an early advocate of nonsectarian education supported by public funding. His classes, moreover, were graded and organized through the monitorial system or what we now know as peer teaching.

Lancaster also developed the concept of simultaneous instruction, and he integrated the subject matter, a predecessor of whole language education. In addition to these innovations were his ideas on written examinations, quantitative assessment, and a new form of discipline that was built around the concept of praise and rewards on the one hand, and shame and humiliation on the other.

Nonsectarian Education

While Lancaster was a deeply religious man who had embraced Quakerism at an early age, he also recognized that his students had diverse religious and nonreligious beliefs as well as different ethnic and cultural backgrounds. As a result, Lancaster promoted Christian morality in a nonsectarian context.

As we have seen, this approach was a distinct shift from traditional religious education both in Europe and in the new United States. For example, early New England Puritan schools, often seen as the first system of "public education" in the American colonies, were not "public" at all but centered on the religious values and the teachings of Calvinism. Non-Puritan children need not apply!

While Lancaster's approach was challenged by churchmen throughout this period, "pan Protestant" education would become the norm in the United States by the first decades of the nineteenth century.

D. P. Page, the great educator and pedagogue of this era, wrote that "we are dependent . . . on the life-giving truths of Protestant Christianity. However, when I say religious training, I do not mean sectarianism. There is a common ground we can occupy." In short, Lancaster's "outrageous" nonsectarian approach to education soon would become the norm in common schools throughout the United States.

Public Funding of Schools

And yet, as a result of Lancaster's idealistic approach to teaching the poor and his rejection of sectarian church support, he had a lifelong struggle to keep his schools in operation. He typically relied on philanthropy and spent most of his time securing funding for his schools. He often found himself in financial trouble and once was jailed in a debtors' prison.

Ironically, Lancaster's financial difficulties became an important lesson for future educators. Horace Mann, for one, was certainly no supporter of the Lancaster monitorial system but he recognized that only through tax-supported public funding of schools would his noble experiment succeed.

As Secretary of Education of Public Schools, Mann understood that an important part of his job was to alert the people of Massachusetts to the importance of public funding of common schools. As we will see in chapter 5, Mann's *Common School Journal* routinely challenged the arguments against public funding and his powerful response to those who had "funding hesitancy."

The Graded School

One of the pillars of modern education today is the graded school. But until the late eighteenth century most schools were "ungraded." Generally, schools were organized as one class with all the students given the same general assignments to read and memorize. One by one, they would approach the teacher and recite their lessons.

Given the enormous size of Lancaster's schools, however, this approach was not realistic. As a result, Lancaster divided the class into monitorial groups with older, brighter students as "peer teachers." Each of these clusters of 10–12 students was formed from those "whose proficiency (was) on par." Monitors then taught the three basic subjects of reading, writing, and arithmetic, maintained discipline, and assessed each student's progress.

In his *Pocket Manual* published in 1827, Lancaster codified his "system" of standardized pedagogy that allowed both experienced and inexperienced monitors to implement his teaching method. This "standardized" approach, he argued, would help transcend the dramatic variations in teaching style of these young peer teachers.

Whole Language

Embedded in Lancaster's system of education was his application of what we now know as whole language. For example, his lessons effectively combined the language arts skills. As his biographer, David Salmon, remarked, Lancaster "made many . . . improvements in the details of instruction . . . [including] one practice which seems almost an inspiration; he combined the lessons of reading, writing and spelling."

Salmon continued by writing "today (1904) we are hailing 'Correlation' as a blessed gift of the German Herbart." By employing the innovative teaching technique of whole language, Lancaster's monitors were able to present material to their students that was less abstract and more readily understood.

Written Exams and Quantitative Assessment

Another important innovation of Lancaster's monitorial system was the written examination. Since students in each small "class" were exposed to the same material at the same time, monitors were able to assess students' progress more equitably. It also helped to change the social relations of the classroom itself. Bright and hardworking students were rewarded (often with prizes and badges) while poor and "indolent" students were "punished" with some form of mild humiliation.

Show Slates!

Rather than monitors assessing each student through an oral examination, however, written exams that could quantify their progress were employed. Each day, students were examined. The master, often Lancaster himself in the early years, would direct the monitors to dictate words or arithmetic problems that students would write on their slates. When complete, monitors would direct students to "show slates." Students would then be assessed and given a numerical grade.

As Michael Hogan has noted, this form of assessment created "a hierarchical . . . structure of opportunity in which the rate of mobility was determined by meritocratic performance." Today this system of simultaneous instruction, written examinations, and quantitative assessments is the cornerstone of modern schools.

Discipline

Finally, the Lancaster system of education introduced a new and "radical" form of discipline in schools. Combined with the Quaker ideal of nonviolence and his intellectual collaboration with Locke and Rousseau, Lancaster developed a psychological approach to disciplining children.

As we have seen, the conventional method of discipline in both the home and school at this time was often excessive corporal punishment based on the biblical teachings in Proverbs such as "spare the rod and spoil the child." Despite his religious upbringing, Lancaster rejected this approach and used a system of "constant activity and proper motivation."

Rewards and Punishment

To motivate students, Lancaster also used material rewards for outstanding grades, regular attendance, and exceptional behavior. He gave prizes to these students including toys, children's books, medals, silver pins, purses, and badges. These students would be promoted to the next "grade" and then parade around the school, led by a herald who would announce: "These good boys have obtained prizes and are going into another class."

Meanwhile, students who did not attend school regularly, did not complete their lessons, or incessantly talked in class were often punished by wearing a small log around their neck. If students disobeyed their parents or a monitor, used profanity, or were simply "sloven," they might be instructed to wear a sign describing their misbehavior, or wear a simple paper crown (dunce cap) as a form of humiliation.

Other offenses such as "slothfulness" were punished by tying the student to their desk. And if a student arrived at school with dirty hands and face, the punishment was the humiliation of being washed before the class by a girl!

While many of these punishments may seem extreme today, we should remember that the typical method of discipline of this and earlier periods was whipping the student with a ferule, rod, or switch. Nevertheless, Lancaster's biographer David Salmon has noted that "these punishments were varied and curious . . . it is doubtful whether the victim would always prefer them to the rod, the use of [which] they were meant to obviate."

Lancaster's Collaboration

In short, Lancaster's methods of teaching the poor were based on his movement collaboration with the Quaker community as well as intellectual collaboration with Enlightenment and pre-Enlightenment philosophers such as John Locke, Voltaire, Jean-Jacques Rousseau, and others. His sense of humanitarianism and determination to teach the poor were nurtured by his religious faith, while some of his ideas on discipline and teaching in general were formed by his close study of a handful of foundationalist philosophers.

Lancaster's Growing Reputation

Lancaster's Borough Road School was a humble establishment, operating on a shoestring budget. He taught children who were often seen as the "refuse of society," and as a result his reputation grew among educators throughout England. With the publication of his pamphlet "Improvements in Education as It Relates to the Industrious Classes of the Community" in 1803, however, his standing grew to include politicians and even King George III of England.

It was at this point in his career that Lancaster began to focus less on teaching and more on promoting his educational "system." He traveled throughout England, lecturing on education and the importance of his monitorial approach. So successful were these lectures that he was given a special audience with the King.

Praise for His Methods

Lancaster gained further notoriety when in 1806, James Pillans, Rector of Edinburgh High School, praised his system and wrote that Lancaster had "converted a laborious and often irksome profession (i.e., teaching) into the most easy and delightful employment possible."

A year later, in 1807, Lancaster was recognized by Samuel Whitbread, a member of the House of Commons. Whitbread, a brewer, abolitionist, and fierce advocate for the poor had introduced a bill in Parliament to reform the Poor Laws of England. In his address, he praised Lancaster's system, noting that "just within a few years, Lancaster had discovered a plan of instruction of youth which is now been brought to a state of perfection."

Whitbread continued his praise of Lancaster by saying that his system of education "will furnish a mode of instruction not only for this country but for all nations." Whitbread's words were prophetic. The young and rather humble educator suddenly had gained international recognition.

Lancaster Lectures Abroad

As a result of his growing reputation, Lancaster began lecturing throughout France, Sweden, Denmark, Russia, and Switzerland. Then, in 1818, he traveled to New York City at the invitation of the New York Public School Society. His trip was sponsored by Robert Vaux, a Philadelphia Quaker and abolitionist. In New York Lancaster lectured extensively, and soon his work caught the attention of Dewitt Clinton, then governor of New York.

Lancaster in the United States

Governor Clinton greatly admired Lancaster's system and helped him establish a number of schools in New York City. Clinton also saw to it that Lancaster was honored and was "seated" in New York's State House of Representatives where he received both praise and notoriety.

Lancaster then traveled to Philadelphia and, with the continued financial support of Quaker Robert Vaux, established a model school to train teachers in his "system." After an unsuccessful attempt to establish a school in Baltimore, Lancaster traveled to New Haven, Connecticut, and founded yet another large monitorial school.

International Reputation

By the mid-1820s Lancaster, still in his early 40s, had achieved an international reputation. Hundreds of educators from throughout the world regularly came to the Borough Road School to observe his new and innovative form of teaching. Among those who visited in 1818 was the renowned revolutionary leader Simón Bolívar, often referred to as the "George Washington of South America."

Bolívar and Lancaster

Bolívar was so impressed with the Borough Road School that he sent two trusted lieutenants to London to study the monitorial system. For his part, Lancaster recognized an opportunity to establish schools in South America. During a brief stay in Baltimore, he met one of Bolívar's Irish Legion lieutenants, Brooke Young. Lancaster persuaded Young to personally deliver a letter to Bolívar indicating his interest in establishing schools in Colombia.

Bolívar was humbled by Lancaster's overture and invited him to Colombia and promised him an enormous grant of $20,000 to establish schools in his country. This grant amounted to nearly a half million dollars in today's currency and, as expected, Lancaster was overwhelmed. Financial security now seemed possible for the first time in his life.

Lancaster in Colombia

Lancaster literally dropped everything and made arrangements to travel to Caracas, then part of Colombia. He and his entire family left the United States and after a rather arduous journey landed in La Guaira en route to the capitol city.

The Lancasters arrived in Caracas in May 1824 to a warm reception by Bolívar and his entourage. Once he was settled, Lancaster sent for his fiancée, Mary Robinson of Philadelphia. Mary was the wealthy widow of John Robinson, the renowned artist of miniature portraits. She made the journey to Caracas, and soon they were married.

Their wedding was a lavish affair. Bolívar himself presided over the ceremony and as might be expected, it was held in one of Lancaster's classrooms with a number of his finest students in attendance. High-ranking officers in the revolutionary guard, members of the nobility, and wealthy merchants from all over Colombia were guests at this luxurious event.

Schools in Mexico

Meanwhile Lancaster's reputation had spread to Mexico where he was hailed as a visionary. In 1822, three of his former students opened a school in Mexico, drafted rules based on the Lancastrian method, and founded the *Compania Lancasteriana de Mexico*. Then, in 1825, Lancaster sent his daughter, Betsy, and her husband, Richard Madox Jones, to Mexico to manage the schools.

Richard was a skilled educator and quite capable in his new position. He had been trained at the Borough Road School by Lancaster himself in 1812, and then he taught at a number of schools in Godalming and Cornwall, England. Eventually Richard became a part of the Lancaster household and traveled with the family to the United States and later to Colombia. Richard and Betsy were married in 1824.

Their work was quite successful and in just a few years, the number of Lancastrian schools in Mexico had grown dramatically. These schools were so successful that in 1843, the Federal Directorate of Public Instruction formally organized them as the basis of Mexico's public education system that lasted for the rest of the nineteenth century.

Problems in Columbia

Lancaster did establish several schools in Colombia and, since he did not speak the language, he recruited bilingual students as his monitors. And yet progress was slow. His own language difficulties eventually proved to be an overwhelming problem and the promised funding from Bolívar was not forthcoming.

Forced to Flee Colombia

Soon however, things began to completely unravel for Lancaster and his family. His inability to speak Spanish and his rather abrasive personality soon doomed his hopes for a secure financial future in Colombia. Moreover, the promised grant of $20,000 never materialized. This put a strain on his relations with Bolívar, and in April 1827 Lancaster and his family fled the country in the dead of night.

The Lancasters traveled through the "sugar islands" of the Caribbean and arrived in New Haven in June. He then dispatched Mary and her three children back to Philadelphia.

Success in Canada

Once settled, Lancaster sent for his family and together they decided to return to England by way of Canada. But while in Quebec, he realized that there was strong support for his teaching methods in the region. In fact, Lancaster's reputation in Canada had been growing for a number of years and monitorial schools had been established there as early as 1814.

As a result of this notoriety, he traveled and lectured widely, visiting schools throughout lower Canada. He was even offered a position as editor of a new *Journal of Education*, though that project never fully materialized.

School for "Backward Children"

Then, one his most ardent supporters, Louis-Joseph Papineau, Speaker of the House of Assembly, arranged for Lancaster to receive a sizable grant from the Legislature of Lower Canada to establish a school for "backward children."

Excited by the prospect, Lancaster traveled to Montreal and organized a school in his home on Rue St-Jacques with the help of his stepchildren. He began with 30 students and in a matter of months nearly doubled that number. These "backward children" soon were making considerable progress, with many learning to read.

Return to New York and Early Death

But just as the school was experiencing real progress, the region endured a major cholera outbreak. As a result, all plans were put on hold and the school was closed. Lancaster then returned to the New York where, with the support of a several prominent Quakers, he was able to continue work on his new book, *Epitome of Some of the Chief Events and Transactions: Containing an Account of the Rise and Progress of the Lancastrian System of Education.*

His book was published, and Lancaster gained new enthusiasm for education. He even made plans to return to England to train more monitors in his system. Lancaster wrote that with his system he could "teach ten thousand children in different schools, not knowing their letters, all to read fluently in three weeks to three months." Tragically, on an early October morning, he was struck by a runaway horse and carriage, run over, and killed. Joseph Lancaster was just 59 years old.

CRITICISMS OF LANCASTER

The great educator was flawed. During his life, some argued that Lancaster was insane. And today a few scholars suggest that he may have been bipolar. Whatever his psychological state, he clearly was difficult to work with and could be abrasive to both colleagues and critics. Many were repelled by his conceit.

His biographer David Salmon, for example, wrote that "Lancaster was a man who, if he had only found out for himself the advantage of tying a knot on the end of a thread, would have proclaimed aloud that he had made an original discovery destined to regenerate society and would have elaborated a complete scheme of knots for different threads or different kinds of sewing."

Criticism of Lancaster's System

Others avoided personal attacks and openly criticized his "system." Early on, J. B. Hutton, a schoolmaster from Albany, New York, pleaded with Governor DeWitt Clinton to abandon his support of Lancaster's system, noting that while it may have been appropriate for simple ideas, it was less useful for more complex ones.

Hutton went on to say, "The alphabet is indeed taught with great clarity; and I am satisfied that . . . elementary arithmetic may thus be acquired; or anything merely practical or mechanical, but that which requires the exercise of judgement, I never knew to be taught through the medium of monitors with certainty or success."

Criticism by Religious Leaders

The religious community also was critical of Lancaster's approach. Salmon noted that its "cheapness delighted them (and its) efficiency surprised them, but its excellence in these respects only made it more dangerous—for it was unsectarian."

One church leader, Mrs. Sarah Trimmer, called Lancaster "a Goliath." She went on to say that "of all the plans that have appeared in this kingdom likely to supplant the church, Mr. Lancaster seems to me the most formidable."

Horace Mann's Criticism

Horace Mann (see chapter 5) also was critical of Lancaster's system, especially his use of monitors. In his *Report on the Educational Tour in Germany*, published in 1846, Mann wrote "One must see the difference between the hampering . . . instruction given by an inexperienced child (monitor) and the developing, transforming and almost creative power of an accomplished teacher."

LANCASTER: A PRODUCT OF COLLABORATION

Joseph Lancaster was the product of both intellectual collaboration with the foundationalists and movement collaboration with the Society of Friends. He clearly was influenced by the work of John Locke and Jean-Jacques Rousseau, especially their ideas on discipline and the need to abandon corporal punishment of children. And from the enlightenment scholars Voltaire, Rousseau, and others, he favored a separation of church and state and a nonsectarian approach to education.

From the Quakers, Lancaster clearly was moved by the abominable condition of enslaved Africans and their lack of freedom and education. His idealistic attempt at the age of 14 to travel to the West Indies to teach the enslaved is a testament to his humanitarianism. And his "free monitorial" schools, designed to teach the "new poor" throughout England and then internationally, reveal his enduring sense of both charity and generosity.

Despite his flawed character and criticism from his peers, Lancaster's pedagogical approach has had a lasting legacy on education. As we have seen, his market-based system, his desire for public funding of schools, his graded classes, his peer teaching, simultaneous instruction, written exams, quantitative assessment, whole language, disciplinary methods, and nonsectarian schools have been adopted in one form or fashion in modern schools throughout the nation.

Lancaster's direct intellectual association with the Enlightenment spirit of the eighteenth century, his movement collaboration with the Friends with their powerful humanitarianism, and his activist impulse to help the poor matched with an incredible pragmatic educational entrepreneurial spirit changed our vision of education.

Chapter 3

Education for Democracy

As reformers began to recognize the need to uplift the poor through education, a new democratic revolution was sweeping through the American colonies. Linked intellectually to the ideas and writings of Enlightenment figures in Europe, Founding Fathers such as Thomas Jefferson, Benjamin Franklin, and Benjamin Rush collaborated to create a new educational system that would support their democratic experiment.

THOMAS JEFFERSON

Thomas Jefferson was a true child of the Enlightenment. His education was rooted in the Enlightenment spirit of the day. At the age of five he began his education by learning the alphabet and numbers at a local school. Four years later at the age of nine he began his studies under the tutelage of "Mr.

Figure 3.1. Thomas Jefferson's image of the Academical Village, University of Virginia. Engraving by William Goodacre and Fenner Sears & Co., 1831. http://www2.iath.virginia.edu/wilson/uva/uva.html.

Douglas." Jefferson would recall later that Douglas was a "clergyman from Scotland (who) was but a superficial Latinist, less instructed in Greek but (along) with the rudiments of these languages he taught me French."

Early Training

When Jefferson was 14 years old, he began his studies under James Maury. Maury was a graduate of William and Mary College and was classically trained. Nevertheless, his approach to teaching was primarily to introduce the young Jefferson to the manners and customs of a gentleman in the Virginia gentry rather than emphasizing classical studies. Jefferson studied with Maury for two years.

Jefferson read the classics under Maury and was especially interested in Cicero's *Tusculum*, which centered on the inevitability of death. This was understandable because his father had recently died. But Jefferson was not particularly interested in the Roman orators; rather, he preferred the historians Tacitus, Livy, and Sallust.

William and Mary

Fresh from his classical studies with Maury, Jefferson entered William and Mary College at the age of 16. At that time, however, the college was in turmoil. One of his professors, Jacob Rowe, was a young, outspoken firebrand who had made "scandalous remarks" regarding members of the Virginia House of Burgesses. Rowe was sued, forced to formally apologize and to pay considerable court costs.

Another one of his professors, Goronwy Owen, was equally disruptive and was described by Jefferson as a "drunk and a brawler." As might be expected, Rowe and Owen became fast friends and drinking buddies. At one point, the two incited a riot with locals outside a pub and encouraged students to join in the melee. Rowe and Owen were fired as a result of this incident.

The Scottish Enlightenment

Throughout these tumultuous times, Jefferson turned to a more serious scholar, William Small, for his studies. Small graduated from Mariscal College in Scotland and had been appointed as the Philosophical Chair at William and Mary shortly after Jefferson's arrival. It was through Professor Small's direction that Jefferson received his serious introduction to the ideas of the Scottish Enlightenment.

Jefferson historian Ralph Ketcham (1984) has noted that Jefferson's intellectual development was a product of "the basic influence . . . of Hutcheson,

Thomas Reed, Adam Smith and other Scottish Enlightenment figures." The connection between the Scottish Enlightenment and the intellectual development of Thomas Jefferson and other Founding Fathers of the American Revolution cannot be overstated.

By the early eighteenth century, Scotland had become a modern nation. Its intellectual development began during the Protestant Reformation when its leaders embraced a form of Calvinism that eventually became the Presbyterian Church.

The Scottish Educational System

This Presbyterian ethos centered on literacy so that their congregants could read the Bible. In 1661, the church mandated that every town have a schoolmaster educated in Latin for the instruction of brighter older children and that rural parishes maintain primary schools. This policy had a dramatic effect on the literacy of Scotsmen. By 1750, it has been estimated that nearly three-quarters of the adult population of Scotland were literate compared to only half of the adults in England.

Edinburgh and Glasgow

Paralleling this growing literacy was an intellectual revolution at the university level in Scotland. The University of Edinburgh and the University of Glasgow became centers of scholarly activity, fostering new modern approaches in economics through the work of Adam Smith and geology through the research of James Hutton, the "father of modern geology." Incidentally, James Watt invented the steam engine in Scotland and helped launch the Industrial Revolution. Moreover, the *Encyclopedia Britannica* was first published in Edinburgh.

Both universities broke from university tradition by embracing specialization. Rather than each professor teaching all the courses within the curriculum, as was the case with Oxford and Cambridge, these schools recruited specialists for specific courses. Today, this is standard curricular approach for universities.

In addition, both universities became meritocratic institutions by the early eighteenth century. Unlike Oxford and Cambridge, where tuition was out of the reach of both middle class and poorer students, tuition at Edinburgh and Glasgow was about one-tenth that of these premier English universities. As historian Thomas E. Ricks has noted, the great philosopher, mathematician, and historian Thomas Carlyle was able to enroll in the University of Edinburgh by simply "walking eighty miles to the city and presenting himself."

The meritocratic orientation and modern curricular focus of these schools was enhanced by the fact that both institutions were culturally diverse. Students from Russia, Portugal, France, and other nations came to Edinburgh and Glasgow to study. The effect of this diversity was dramatic, especially in the area of law.

Rather than embracing English common law, these universities gradually aligned with French jurisprudence that had its roots in Roman law, especially the Codex of Emperor Justinian I. This important connection encouraged Scottish legal scholars to emphasize classical principles and reason rather than common law. The great Scottish jurist Lord Kames once wrote, "our law is grafted on that of old Rome."

Scottish Law and Jefferson

Under the tutelage of the Scotsman William Small, Jefferson was introduced to Lord Kames and his translation of the Justinian Codex. In fact, Jefferson hand-copied more than 30,000 words from this document into his personal notebook. This had a profound impact on the young scholar who would be shaped by the philosophy and legal traditions of classical Rome.

Scottish Economic Connections to Virginia

The intellectual connection between the Scottish Enlightenment and the British colonies was not only a product of the scholars who came to America to teach; there also was a direct economic connection between Scotland and the colonies.

In 1707, the English Act of Union united Scotland, England, and Wales. As a result, Scottish merchants were introduced to Virginia tobacco and soon became major importers of the prized weed. Within a decade, this commerce connection had stimulated the economies of both Scotland and the Virginia colony. In fact, by 1760, Glasgow imported more tobacco than all English ports combined.

This economic connection also led to the immigration of many scholars to the New World. One particularly important figure was James Blair from Edinburgh. In the 1670s Blair immigrated to Virginia and played an important role in the establishment of William and Mary College in 1693. Blair served as president of the school for many years.

The eighteenth century also witnessed the immigration of hundreds of Scottish graduates from Glasgow and Edinburgh to Virginia. These individuals played a major role in the intellectual development of the colony. As Daniel Defoe wrote in a travelog on Scotland in the 1720s, "if it (immigration) holds on for many years more, Virginia may rather be called a Scots rather than an English plantation."

Books Imported from Scotland

The impact of the Scottish Enlightenment on the American founding fathers also was reinforced by the importation of hundreds of thousands of books from Scotland. Ships sailing from Scotland to Virginia and other colonies often packed their holds with books as their primary cargo. On the return voyage, these same ships would be loaded with tobacco.

The Foulis Brothers Press of Glasgow was the leading publishing house and supplier of classical literature in English. These volumes were typically leather-bound, and the brothers prided themselves in providing the most accurate translation of the classical masters available.

Influence on Jefferson

These editions, moreover, were Jefferson's favorites. He collected them and proudly displayed them in his office. Later he praised the Foulis Brothers' volumes for their "perfection of accuracy." Jefferson went on to say that "I have understood they offered 1,000 Guineas for the discovery of any error in it."

Jefferson was profoundly influenced by the Scottish Enlightenment. It was Scottish empiricism integrated with commonsense realism that influenced him throughout his life. In addition to scientific observation, Jefferson also relied on his "senses" to understand the world.

Jefferson Studies Law

Fully engaged with the philosophies of Scottish empiricism and commonsense realism, Jefferson turned to the study of law with George Wythe. Jefferson would later write that this "was one of the most fortunate events of his life."

Wythe was one of the foremost scholars of classical law, and he instructed Jefferson in the classical rather than the English common law traditions that were pervasive throughout the colonies. This gave Jefferson a unique understanding of his chosen profession, and later he wrote that his work with Wythe was "his real education."

Elected to the House of Burgesses

After several years of reading the law with Wythe, Jefferson began a short career as an attorney in 1767. Within just two years, however, he was elected to the House of Burgesses. Here he would articulate his ideas regarding the importance of education. Clearly, Jefferson's training in philosophy and the law provided a firm foundation for his nation-building efforts as well as his work in the field of education.

Importance of Education

As a result of his broad classical training embedded in the ideas of the Scottish Enlightenment, Jefferson was convinced that if our democratic republic were to survive, an educated public was necessary. Bill 79, presented to the Virginia Assembly in 1778, clearly stated that "even under the best forms, those entrusted with power have, in time and by slow operations, perverted it into tyranny." The only solution to this paradox of democracy was an educated public that would elect honorable and able leaders.

Later Jefferson would demonstrate the importance of education in the new republic by noting that "whenever the people are well informed, they can be trusted with their own government; that whenever things get so far wrong as to attract their notice, they may be relied on to set them to rights." This, of course, is an important lesson today.

Bill 79

To achieve this goal, Jefferson proposed in his Bill 79 a three-tiered system of education for the people of Virginia and, by extension, the American people. It provided for three years of primary education for both boys and girls. Then, a select number of young men would receive advanced studies, with one boy from each district awarded a scholarship to William and Mary College.

Although his system favored the education of boys, except at the primary level, Jefferson did understand the importance of educating women. In a letter to Nathaniel Burwell in 1818, he recommended a more informal approach for their studies. Jefferson wrote that it was "essential to give them a solid education which might enable them, when they become mothers, to educate their own daughters and even to direct the course for sons."

While Bill 79 is now widely recognized as a bedrock principle of democracy, it was rejected by the House of Delegates of the Virginia Assembly in 1778 and again in 1780. Finally, under the leadership of James Madison, the revised bill was passed into law in 1796 as an "Act to Establish Public Schools."

Higher Education Advocate

In addition to his support of primary and secondary education, Jefferson also was a leading advocate for higher education owing to his work establishing the University of Virginia. This premier institution was conceived as a college that would not only cater to the rich and powerful in Virginia society, but would also welcome talented young Americans irrespective of their social class.

Jefferson had lost confidence in his alma mater, William and Mary, throughout the years. The tumultuous period during his residency at the school, the college's requirement that students recite the catechism daily, and its tacit rejection of the sciences convinced him that the college was in decline and a new approach to higher education was necessary.

Collaboration at the University of Virginia

In 1817, Jefferson collaborated with a distinguished group of statesmen, jurists, and other dignitaries to discuss the creation of a new modern college. After some deliberation, the group chose Charlottesville as the site for the school and purchased land from James Monroe to erect the college.

Construction began that same year and the first classes were held in March 1825. Unlike other colleges of the day, students were given the opportunity to study one or more of the eight disciplines at the school: medicine, law, mathematics, chemistry, ancient languages, modern languages, natural philosophy, and moral philosophy. A school of engineering and applied science opened in 1836, the first of its kind in the United States.

Secular Education

In addition, the University of Virginia embraced secular education. It was a public university with no affiliation to a religious sect and no divinity school on campus. Interestingly, Virginia was not positioned around a church, as were most schools at the time, but rather centered around a library. Jefferson underscored the secular nature of the university in a letter to Thomas Cooper and wrote "a professorship of theology shall have no place in our institution."

Academical Village

The University of Virginia was in many ways a reflection of Jefferson's educational background and ideals. He conceived of a school that would embrace "discussion, collaboration and enlightenment." The school was designed as an "academical village." Faculty lived in houses surrounded by a central lawn, with student residents situated between faculty homes. The library or rotunda was placed at the head of the lawn.

This unique landscape architecture was designed to promote informal exchanges between faculty and students and also a collaborative environment where both students and faculty learned from one another.

Thomas Jefferson insisted that his gravestone should mention only his authorship of the Declaration of Independence and the Virginia Statute of Religious Freedom, and the Father of the University of Virginia. Clearly, his support of education at the primary, secondary, and university level set the standard for the future of education in America and demonstrated its central importance for the maintenance of democracy.

Collaboration

And yet, Jefferson was not alone in these educational efforts. As we have seen, he collaborated with members of the House of Burgesses to promote legislation for his famous Bill 79. Moreover, his close colleague, James Monroe, was a formal collaborator who made changes in the bill and helped to push it through the Virginia Assembly in 1796. This collaborative work led to one of the earliest models for truly public, primary and secondary education in the United States.

Jefferson also collaborated with dozens of dignitaries in the design and development of the University of Virginia during the early nineteenth century. Among these important figures were two presidents of the United States, James Monroe and James Madison; Chief Justices of the Supreme Court; and twenty-four other luminaries. Later, when the University opened, several of these individuals served on the Board of Visitors. Clearly, it was the close collaboration between Jefferson and his trusted colleagues that created this educational vision for the new republic.

BENJAMIN FRANKLIN

While Jefferson's educational contributions were enormous, his colleague, Benjamin Franklin, was perhaps equally as important. Unlike Jefferson, who had the benefit of a "gentleman's education," Franklin was for the most part self-educated and apprenticed.

Benjamin Franklin was born in Boston in 1706, the tenth son of a tallow chandler and soap maker. Each of his brothers had become apprentices at an early age, but Benjamin was seen as having "special abilities" and was enrolled in a grammar school at the age of eight with the idea that he would become a minister.

Early Education

Benjamin attended the Boston Latin school for two years but was forced to leave when his father had financial difficulties. He then returned home to help his father in the trade. Soon, however, he was able to continue his education and was placed with George Brownell, a tutor, to learn writing and arithmetic. Benjamin's skill as a writer was apparent at an early age, but he had little interest in arithmetic and failed the subject miserably.

Apprenticeship

At the age of 12, Benjamin was apprenticed to his brother, James, in the printing trade. It was here that his real education began. He read everything that crossed his desk, from the secular writings of John Locke and Daniel Defoe to the religious parables of John Bunyan and the sermons of Cotton Mather.

Then, in 1721, James founded the *New England Courant*, one of the first newspapers published in the British Colonies. This was a turning point in young Benjamin's life. He wanted to publish a series of letters in the newspaper, but James thought better of it, arguing that he was simply too young for such a project.

Mrs. Silence Dogood

Benjamin, however, was determined and published a series of 14 letters under the pseudonym "Mrs. Silence Dogood!" These letters became a sensation in Boston. In his first two letters, for example, he introduced the reading public to Silence Dogood with "thrilling" stories of her early life, apprenticeship to a pious country minister, education, daily life, marriage, and widowhood. Other letters chronicled Dogood's life and helped Benjamin hone his skills as a journalist of sorts.

Philadelphia

Apparently bored with Boston, Benjamin left his apprenticeship and ran away to Philadelphia to begin a new chapter of his life. He worked in a number of printing shops but was unhappy with these positions. Eventually he ended up in London, where he learned typesetting, and then at the age of 20 he returned to Philadelphia.

The Junto

Within a year, Franklin established his famous Junto, a group of artisans and tradesmen who sought to improve themselves and their community. The Junto was modeled after the coffeehouses that Franklin had observed while in London.

The group routinely read and discussed the new ideas of the Enlightenment and created a small library to share their books. This concept became the basis of Franklin's subscription library in 1731, known officially as the Library Company of Philadelphia. This system of lending libraries would be an important educational cornerstone of the new republic.

Pennsylvania Gazette

Meanwhile, Franklin's mentor and financial benefactor, Thomas Denham, passed away in 1728 and presumably left him with a small inheritance. Franklin used this money to establish his own printing house. The following year he began publishing the *Pennsylvania Gazette*. This newspaper, along with his *Poor Richards Almanack*, was a great success and provided him with financial stability as well as a forum to present his own political ideas.

By his early 40s Franklin had become a successful and wealthy businessman. He now had time for his scientific experiments in electricity with his famous and dangerous "kite and key" exercise in 1752. The result of these experiments led to the invention of the lightning rod.

Later, he would map the Gulf Stream, identify the cause of the Aurora Borealis, develop the basis of meteorology, suggest the roots of the common cold, and recognize the cause of lead poisoning. He also would invent bifocals and a new heating device now known as the Franklin Stove.

Franklin's Ideas on Education

But beyond these important scientific experiments and inventions, Franklin, Like Jefferson, was an educational activist. Interestingly, Franklin also embraced what we now recognize as the movement from memorization to understanding. He noted that "our boys read as parrots speak, knowing little or nothing of the meaning."

Franklin had long supported academies, professional schools, and colleges for women. Like Jefferson and most of the Enlightenment figures of this period, Franklin rejected what was called "the doctrine of innate ideas." As we have seen, this was the notion that people were essentially born with innate knowledge derived from God. As a result, there were a few great geniuses, and most people were simply uneducable in the higher orders of learning.

Like Jefferson, Franklin also was an "environmentalist" who believed that all young people could be trained and educated. Similarly, Franklin saw education as the basis of a successful democratic republic. In a letter to his friend Samuel Adams in 1750, Franklin articulated this idea when he wrote: "I think with you that nothing is more important for the public weal than to form and train up youth in wisdom and virtue . . . wise and good men are in my opinion, the strength of the state, much more so than riches or arms."

The Academy

For years, Franklin had envisioned a school for young boys in Philadelphia. Then, in 1749, he wrote "Proposals Relating to the Education of Youth in Pennsylvania." This article recommended a school be established that would introduce students to academic subjects and also provide them with practical skills for their future occupations.

Students studying for the ministry or medicine, for example, would learn the classical languages of Greek and Latin, while those becoming merchants would focus on "living languages" such as English, French, Spanish, and German. In addition, all students would be exposed to a general education component including agriculture, mechanics, the natural sciences, arithmetic, accounting, geometry, astronomy, grammar, writing, public speaking, and history.

Franklin collaborated with a group of wealthy merchants and professionals who formally established the Academy in 1751, using Franklin's "Constitution of the Publick Academy" as its foundation. The 24 original founding trustees saw the purpose of the Academy as providing moral and economic benefits for the young men of Philadelphia.

The College of Philadelphia

Two years later, a Charity School under the auspices of the Academy was established. Then, in 1755, the school added an undergraduate component to the growing institution known as the College of Philadelphia. All three schools had the same trustees and were part of the expanding educational complex.

Early Struggles with the Academy

The original Academy consisted of two "divisions"—Latin and English. Bright boys were accepted as students and charged one pound per quarter. The course of study began with languages and then proceeded to history, logic, writing, and mathematics.

The struggle to create a school that was secular and centered on the study of modern languages, however, was ongoing. Franklin himself designed the English division of the Academy that focused on writing, oratory, and modern English literature. The Latin division was led by George Whitefield, a noted revivalist preacher. Whitefield, however, clashed with Franklin and eventually attempted to combine the curriculum of both divisions to center on the classics.

Franklin also clashed with the provost of the Academy, William Smith, who attempted to move the school toward a more religious, Friends orientation. This idea also was supported by the Penn Family Proprietors. In a 1756 letter to Peter Collinson, Franklin condemned both the Quaker "stiffrumps" and William Smith's support of them. But despite these ongoing problems and clashes, the original vision of the Academy persisted and provided a unique model of modern, secular, secondary education in the colonies.

The University of Pennsylvania

Meanwhile, the original College of Philadelphia was expanding; however, in 1779, during the heat of the Revolutionary War, the legislature of Pennsylvania, unsure of the loyalties of Provost Reverend William Smith, established a separate University of the State of Pennsylvania. For the next decade the two institutions operated separately until they were merged in 1791, to form the University of Pennsylvania.

By then, Franklin had passed, but many of his ideas persisted. This new institution became the fourth oldest college/university in the new United States and was the first to have both graduate and undergraduate studies. With his original Academy, the Charity School, and now the prestigious University of Pennsylvania, Franklin's vision of an educational ladder had been realized.

Women's Education

In addition to his impact on education with his Academy, Charity School, and the University of Pennsylvania, Franklin also was an advocate of schools for women. As early as 1750, Franklin wrote his famous pamphlet "Reflections on Courtship and Marriage," where he argued that women should receive an education similar to that of men. He noted that because of their lack of access to education, many women were undereducated and, as a result, were "courted with flattery and nonsense."

Through education however, women would become as "sensible and reasonable" as men. Although his words may appear a bit demeaning, Franklin's advocacy of female education was an important early step toward gender equity.

Education of Slaves

Similarly, Franklin forcefully argued that the prevailing vision of the enslaved as being inherently inferior and uneducable was a product of misguided thinking based, once again, on the doctrine of innate ideas. In 1763, he visited the "Negro School of Philadelphia" and was impressed with the educational progress that was being made. He noted that in many ways, these children were "equal to that of white children."

Legacy

In short, Franklin's contributions to education were immense. Not only was he instrumental in establishing libraries, schools, and learned societies, he also promoted universal education, including female and black education. His rejection of the doctrine of "innate ideas" moreover helped to cement the idea of secular education for generations to come.

BENJAMIN RUSH

Finally, Benjamin Rush must also be remembered as an important collaborator for democratic education. Unlike some of his more secular-oriented colleagues, however, Rush embraced religious education as an appropriate way to raise young children from "depravity." Reading the Bible then was a central component of education for young children.

Advocate of Universal Education

Despite his differences from the deist Jefferson and the agnostic Franklin, Benjamin Rush was a realist when it came to the importance of education for the maintenance of the democratic republic. Only through universal education, he argued, could the common man become a "republican machine" who could understand the basic principles of democracy.

In fact, Rush argued for compulsory public education, the training of schoolteachers, colleges in each state, and a national university to educate exceptional students in politics and international affairs. Each of the components of his plan would be supported by the people themselves through taxation.

Early Life

Benjamin Rush was born on December 24, 1746, just outside Philadelphia in the township of Byberry. Benjamin's father died when he was only five years old, and his mother supported him and his six siblings by running a country store.

At the age of eight he was sent to live with his aunt and uncle and there he attended a small academy where he was instructed by Reverend Samuel Finley. Under Finley's guidance, Rush received a strict religious education. After several years of study, he enrolled in the College of New Jersey—now Princeton University—and, in 1760, at the age of 14, he received his bachelor of arts degree.

Rush returned to Philadelphia to study medicine under Dr. John Redmond. After six years of apprenticeship, he was encouraged to attend medical school at Edinburgh, Scotland, where he earned a degree in medicine after two years of study. In addition to his medical studies, Rush became fluent in French, Italian, and Spanish. He continued his studies in London at St. Thomas Hospital where he met Benjamin Franklin.

In 1769, at the age of 24, Rush returned to Philadelphia and opened his first medical practice and became a professor of chemistry at Franklin's College of Philadelphia. During this period, Rush also wrote extensively about medical procedures, published a book on chemistry, and became a social activist interested in politics and the abolition of slavery. Thrust into the volatile world of politics, Rush met and collaborated with Thomas Jefferson, John Adams, Thomas Paine, and others.

Revolutionary Philadelphia

Soon, Rush was drawn into the growing controversy concerning the excess taxation of the Stamp Act and the suppression of human rights by the British. He also became a member of the Sons of Liberty. It was here that he gained a greater understanding of the revolutionary cause and the coming war for independence. When the Stamp Act was repealed, the group disbanded, but many of the Sons of Liberty including Rush became active supporters of the American Revolution.

As tension continued to grow in the colonies, in the early 1770s Rush became a revolutionary activist and then a prominent member of the First and Second Continental Congresses of 1774 and 1775 held in Philadelphia.

1776

The year 1776 was a momentous one for Rush. Not only did he become one of the signatories of the Declaration of Independence in July, but in January of that year he married Julia Stockton, daughter of Richard Stockton, another signer of the Declaration of Independence. The couple had 13 children, 9 of whom survived infancy.

This connection, as well as his collaboration with some of the towering figures in the coming struggle, solidified Rush's position as a revolutionary figure. When the war with England broke out, he joined the revolutionary army as a medical officer and surgeon. The following year he was appointed Surgeon General of the Continental Army.

But Rush's career in the military was short. He was appalled by the conditions of the medical service, and he criticized both George Washington and his former professor, Dr. William Shippen, for poor management. As a result of the fallout over this incident, Rush resigned his position as Surgeon General of the Continental Army and returned to his practice in Philadelphia.

Medical Career

Rush spent the last years of the war in his medical practice and was appointed to the staff of the Pennsylvania Hospital. Here he continued his medical writing and teaching. He has been credited with instructing more than 3,000 medical students during his career, including several that established Rush Medical College in Chicago in 1837.

Though his practices such as bleeding, purging, and the use of mercury were repudiated during his lifetime, he contributed to other areas of medicine including the treatment of mental illness and alcoholism. Rush strongly believed in medical freedom and the training of many doctors so that the field would not become a monopoly.

Constitutional Convention

Rush's work in medicine was suspended temporarily when, in 1787, he was elected as a delegate to the Constitutional Convention from Pennsylvania. He played a major role in that body and voted to ratify the U.S. Constitution in 1788. He then served in a variety of governmental capacities and, in 1797, was appointed Treasurer of the United States Mint by John Adams, a position he held until his death in 1813.

Contributions to Education

During these exciting years, Rush also became concerned about the future of the new democratic republic and the role that education would play in its ultimate success. As a strong advocate of higher education, Benjamin Rush was instrumental in establishing Dickinson College in 1783, just days after the signing of the Treaty of Ghent that ended the Revolutionary War.

"Bingham's Porch" Collaboration

Benjamin Rush, James Wilson, William Bingham, and John Montgomery, all prominent political and business leaders in Pennsylvania, met on "Bingham's Porch" in 1782 and planned a new frontier college to be located in Carlisle, Pennsylvania, the westernmost site of a college in the nation at the time. President Dickinson of Pennsylvania gave the school an extensive library and a conservative faculty was recruited, headed by Charles Nisbet, a Scottish minister.

The Educational Ladder

Rush wrote three important pieces on education: first, *Plan for the Establishment of Public Schools* in 1786; the second, *Thoughts upon the Mode of Education Proper in a Republic* published later that year; and *Thoughts upon Female Education* in 1787.

Plan for the Establishment of Public Schools

In his *Plan*, Rush articulated the importance of education for the new Republic. Education, he wrote, would be "friendly to religion, favorable to liberty, it would promote just laws and government, and help to develop both agriculture and manufacturing."

The *Plan* itself had five major structural components that included establishing one university in the state located in Philadelphia, four colleges located in Philadelphia, one in Carlisle (in addition to Dickinson), one in Manheim for German citizens, and one in Pittsburgh. He also recommended that an academy be established in each county in the state to prepare brighter students for college.

Finally, he called for free schools in each township or district of 100 families. Here students would be taught reading, writing, and arithmetic. Rush wrote that in this plan, "the whole state will be tied together by one system of education."

Funding of Education

Rush then addressed funding of his plan, arguing that the sale of public lands would provide adequate revenue for education. In addition, a small tax would be levied on each resident in the county.

For those who feared that taxation would be too steep for the state, Rush wrote that in fact "these institutions are designed to *lessen* our taxes." Education will help the younger residents of the state, the basis of the new emerging economy. And as part of this economic development, profits from both agriculture and manufacturing would increase, as would state tax revenue.

To those married couples who had no children or those who were bachelors and opposed contributing to public education, Rush wrote, "every member of the community (should be) interested in the propagation of virtue and knowledge in the state." Residents "will in time save tax . . . by being able to sleep with fewer bolts and locks to his doors." And there will be "fewer pillories . . . whipping posts and . . . jails with their usual expenses and taxes."

Thoughts upon the Mode of Education

In his *Thoughts upon the Mode of Education* published that same year, Rush expanded on the importance of education for the maintenance of the republic. One of his primary points was that religion *of any kind* was essential in promoting virtue among men. Moreover, he argued that he "must be excused in not agreeing with those modern writers who have opposed the use of the Bible as a schoolbook."

In addition, he wrote that education was essential in a republic where immigrants from throughout Europe had settled. A "common" educational experience was essential to create a homogeneous population that would "fit them more easily for uniform and peaceable government."

Rush also turned to the question of discipline in the nation's classrooms. He wrote "In the education of youth, let the authority of our masters (teachers) be as *absolute* as possible." And yet he cautioned that "the government of schools like the government of private families should (not) be . . . severe."

Thoughts upon Female Education

In his final intellectual contribution to education, Rush turned his attention to women. In his *Thoughts upon Female Education*, published the following year, Rush wrote that "the American Republic is a new phenomenon requiring a new understanding of female education." Since the new economy of the United States often requires men to be away from their families, American women must be able to teach their children both the basics of learning and citizenship.

As a result, the education of women was essential for the new republic. Women "should not only be instructed in the usual branches of female education but . . . [also] in the principles of liberty and government and the obligations of patriotism should be inculcated upon them." Rush concluded by writing that "the opinions and conduct of men are often regulated by the women in the most arduous enterprises of life and their approbation is frequently the principle reward of the hero's dangers and the patriot's toils."

Rush's Legacy

Benjamin Rush died of typhus in 1813, at the age of 68. And yet, his ideas and philosophies have provided generations of scholars and teachers with a blueprint for the future of teaching and education in general. Moreover, his support of public education and his arguments against those who were hesitant to pay taxes for schools were evident in the formation of the common school movement nearly a half a century later.

Rush's understanding of the importance of a common school experience to create a more homogeneous nation from the diverse immigrants coming to this country from throughout Europe, and his ideas on female education, laid a foundation for activists in the nineteenth century and beyond. Finally, his understanding of the importance of education to maintain our democratic republic resonates today.

THREE TITANS

The collaboration of these three titans of the early republic, Thomas Jefferson, Benjamin Franklin, and Benjamin Rush created a foundation for education that would help secure our democracy and provide an inclusive environment for young men, black and white, and for women and adult learners. Together they pushed the boundaries of education for the new nation into the future.

Chapter 4

Gender Equity in Education

Despite the powerful forces of the Enlightenment, the American Revolution, and the work of a number of important Founding Fathers, the educational world of the late eighteenth and early nineteenth centuries continued to be limited for most American women.

Women typically were restricted to a life of domesticity, and they had few legal or financial rights either before or after marriage. Poor white and free black women had no legal rights, while enslaved women were chattel property under the law.

White, middle-class, and farming women could not own property, and, if they did find work outside the household, their wages literally were not their own. Women could not sign contracts and, of course, it would be another century before they achieved the right to vote through the Nineteenth Amendment to the U.S. Constitution.

As a result, most women mastered the lessons of domestic life from their mothers, grandmothers, and older sisters. They learned to cook, sew, tend the kitchen garden, and wash clothes by helping in the household. A few learned to read (in order to read the Bible), but they typically were not taught to write—a skill that was seen as the province of men.

CHANGE COMING, 1787–1821

But change was in the air. In the years between the signing of the U.S. Constitution in 1787 and the second inauguration of James Monroe as president of the United States in 1821, the door to female education opened slightly with the establishment of two institutions. The first was the Young Ladies' Academy of Philadelphia founded in June of 1787, while the second was Emma Willard's Troy Female Seminary founded in the fall of 1821.

Figure 4.1. Emma Willard Seminary, Troy, New York, 1898. Postcard. Photography, Detroit Publishing Company. https://commons.wikimedia.org/wiki/File:Emma_Willard _Seminary,_Troy,_N._Y_(NYPL_b12647398-68636).tiff.

While dozens of female academies and seminaries would follow their lead, affording women an education that was "equal" to that of men, these two schools provided the model for a virtual revolution in female education.

1787

The year 1787 represented a major turning point for the new republic. Just six years before, in October 1781, American and French troops had laid siege to a large British force at Yorktown, Virginia, that culminated with the surrender of British troops and the end of military operations in the United States. Then, in 1783, U.S. and British delegates negotiated the Treaty of Ghent, officially ending America's armed struggle with Britain, securing independence for the thirteen original colonies, and adding significant western territory to the republic.

This enormous increase in the territory was an opportunity for members of the Congress of the Confederation (the first governing body of the new republic) to establish the primacy of the new nation. Congress dealt with land ownership, abolished all state claims to the land, provided for the creation of new states, prohibited slavery in the Northwest Territory, and dealt directly with education.

Northwest Ordinance and Education

Under the provisions of the Northwest Ordinance, Congress called for the establishment of a public university in each state that requested statehood. The provision stated: "Religion, morality and knowledge being necessary to good government and the happiness of mankind, schools and the means of education shall forever be encouraged."

Perhaps more important for education was that, in conjunction with the earlier land ordinance of 1785, a section of each new township was set aside to support schools in that community. New states could sell that land and use the funds derived from the sale to build local schoolhouses and pay teachers. While this provision was not mandated, it did help many communities support education.

YOUNG LADIES' ACADEMY OF PHILADELPHIA

In short, the government under the Congress of the Confederation, with all its limitations and problems, reflected both the age of Enlightenment and the progressive Revolutionary ferment of this period. In many ways, the Young Ladies' Academy of Philadelphia was a reflection of these forces.

The creation of this important institution was a monumental collaboration of political and cultural leaders of the new republic. As we have seen, many of the Founding Fathers felt a responsibility to promote education in this nation for the maintenance of good government. Thomas Jefferson, Benjamin Franklin, and Benjamin Rush, all signatories of the Declaration of Independence, understood their responsibilities in the area of education and established plans for its future.

Changing Attitudes toward Women's Education

This powerful support for education slowly extended to women as well. The spirit of the Enlightenment had begun to change our perspectives regarding female education. Some historians have recognized that there was a shift in attitudes as early as the 1750s toward more practical and formal schooling of women rather than the traditional "education for marriage."

Republican Motherhood

The American Revolution reinforced these new ideas, and women were seen as having an important role in the conflict. Women not only had worked as nurses for the sick and wounded, but also maintained households when the men went off to war. In addition, women played a central role in the education of their children, especially young men. Promoting ideas of patriotism and support for the war was seen as essential to our victory. The concept of "Republican Motherhood" soon became an accepted vision of the importance of female education.

These ideas were given concrete expression by Benjamin Rush in a speech to the newly created Young Ladies' Academy of Philadelphia in 1787. This speech, entitled "Thoughts upon Female Education," set forth a template of ideas on the nature of female education that would provide structure for the school once it was incorporated in 1792.

Rush's speech laid out five aspects of education for women. First, since American women tended to marry young, their education was often cut short. As a result, Rush noted their education should be confined to "the more useful branches of literature." Second, since men depended on "the assistance of the female members of the community," they should be trained to be the "stewards and guardians of their husband's property."

Third, since the business of commerce required men to be away from home a great deal of the time, women were expected to provide for the early education of their children. Indeed, for Rush and other men of this period, the instruction of children (especially their boys) was the most important role of women.

Fourth, related to the preceding point, Rush wrote that since every member of society (including women) would play a central role in preserving the liberty of the new republic, virtue must be promoted. Women therefore needed "to concur in instructing their sons in the principles of liberty and government." Finally, in a point that related specifically to the wealthy members of Philadelphia society, Rush wrote that women must be prepared to handle servants. Servants, he went on to say, needed "good looking after," and that required training.

Proposed Curriculum of the Academy

Rush also outlined subjects to be taught at the Academy. These included a good knowledge of English, both spoken and written. Next came handwriting, with an emphasis on legibility and neatness. Additionally, Rush noted that a knowledge of figures and bookkeeping "was absolutely necessary."

He also recommended other subjects that could be introduced into the curriculum. These included geography and history, astronomy, and philosophy as well as singing and dancing. These subjects would prevent superstition and make a woman an "agreeable companion for a sensible man." Finally, Rush advocated for instruction in Christian religion and principles. For him, this was the most effective means of promoting knowledge and virtue.

The Young Ladies' Academy of Philadelphia was in the planning stage for nearly a decade in the early 1780s. John Poor, a Harvard graduate, was the official "founder" of the institution, and, in 1792, the institution was incorporated by the Pennsylvania legislature. The school was an early success, and, by 1787, it had enrolled more than 100 students.

Collaboration in the Development of the Academy

Although John Poor is credited as "opening" the school, it clearly was a collaborative effort. The trustees of the school were all prominent Philadelphia men—doctors, lawyers, and ministers—each with at least one college degree. Most of the men, moreover, had political experience of some kind.

Benjamin Rush, for example, not only laid out the template for the Academy's curriculum but was a signatory of the Declaration of Independence and was a delegate to both the Continental Congress and the Constitutional Convention. Jared Ingersol, another trustee, also served as a delegate to the Constitutional Convention. Four others were trustees of the University of Pennsylvania, and four more taught at the prestigious institution.

Although not a trustee of the Young Ladies' Academy of Philadelphia, Benjamin Franklin's influence also was clear. The curriculum of the Academy was similar to that of Franklin's Academy of Philadelphia for boys established in 1749. Both schools, for example, placed a great deal of emphasis on competition—what was called emulation. Each semester, the young women competed in public examinations and gave speeches to the trustees. Winners were awarded prizes.

Great Success

The school was a great success and gained a reputation as the premier women's academy in the new United States. One trustee, Benjamin Say, summed up the general feeling of the day when he spoke to the students in 1789. He told the assembled body once again of the great opportunity to receive an education that they had. He noted that other women who had no such opportunity were in a "state of ignorance [and] . . . could not even read their own language with propriety."

Lifting the "Veil of Ignorance"

Students at the Academy seemed to agree wholeheartedly with Benjamin Say's assessment. Ann Loxley, for example, delivered the valedictorian address in June 1790. She noted that women had traditionally been excluded from receiving an education but now, with the Young Ladies' Academy, the "veil of female ignorance" had been lifted.

Other young women praised the educational enlightenment that was now available to them, while others saw it as a liberating experience. Many students, for example, did not see marriage (or childbearing) in their future. Molly Baker encouraged her fellow students to carefully consider not marrying, while others such as Ann Negus noted that many of her classmates would be forced to "resign our liberty" and begin families.

A Challenge to Male Domination

Still other women took a step further and challenged male dominance in public and domestic life. Priscilla Mason, for example, argued that public speaking was an inalienable right promoted by "our high and mighty lords." Mason went on to say that science had proved that women were intellectually equal to men but had been barred from "the Church, the bar and the Senate." Who had done this, she asked rhetorically: "Man; despotic man."

Finally, while most of the women graduates of the Young Ladies' Academy maintained their religious deference, some such as Mason called out the Apostle Paul, "that contemptible little body (who had) declared war against the whole sex." This antipathy to Paul would become an important theme among women's right activists into the nineteenth century and powerfully articulated in the Declaration of Sentiments at the Seneca Falls Convention of 1848.

The influence of the Young Ladies' Academy of Philadelphia cannot be overstated. Not only did it introduce hundreds of women to an education that they would not have had otherwise, but it demonstrated the importance of female education and reminded Americans of the critical role women played in the American Revolution and in domestic life generally.

Momentum Halted

But the Enlightenment spirit that helped to create the Young Ladies' Academy, envisioned schools throughout the nation, and established the means of financing them in the Northwest Territory, essentially was abandoned with the ratification of the U.S. Constitution and the Bill of Rights, especially the Tenth Amendment to the U.S. Constitution.

The Bill of Rights, the first ten amendments to the U.S. Constitution, was of course an attempt by lawmakers to promote a compromise with some state delegates who feared overreach by the federal government. Many of these representatives were concerned that the language of the Constitution did not address individual rights and that it ignored the role of states in the governing process.

The Tenth Amendment, however, was an overly broad measure that gave states great power. The amendment read in part: "The powers not delegated to the United States by the Constitution nor prohibited by it to the States, are reserved to the States respectively, or to the people." Since there was no mention of education in the U.S. Constitution, the states assumed this responsibility.

In many ways, the Tenth Amendment to the U.S. Constitution was a monumental mistake. For American education, however, it was a disaster. States were typically not concerned with education and preferred to continue the practice of allowing churches, tutors, and parents themselves to provide an education for the children of their state. As a result, American education floundered for nearly a half-century after the early 1790s. While education for men was very limited during the early nineteenth century, for women it was virtually nonexistent.

Women's Rights Stalled

In addition, women continued to have few, if any, legal rights. When Emma Willard's husband died in 1825, for example, he bequeathed to her all the copyrights on her *Plan for Improving Female Education* as well as her *The Woodbridge and Willard Geographies and Atlases* because *he* owned these copyrights under law. Moreover, the school property that had been leased to Dr. Willard was turned over to Emma upon his death. Married women could not make a contract, nor could they hold real estate in their own name.

Of course, as we have seen, a number of very lucky women had been able to attend the Young Ladies' Academy of Philadelphia. These women, however, were the exception that proved the rule.

THE WORLD OF EMMA HART WILLARD

It was into this world that Emma Hart was born in 1787. Emma was the 16th of 17 children born to Samuel and Lydia Hart. The large family lived on a farm in Berlin, Connecticut. Samuel was a Revolutionary War veteran and often told stories of his experiences to his brood of children. He also held daily discussions concerning the events and politics of the day and read from the Bible and his modest library.

A Precocious Child

This early exposure to books and reading would have a lasting impact on the young girl, as did Samuel's exciting tales of the Revolutionary War. Emma was a precocious child and soon she had learned to read while sitting on her father's lap. She quickly became the primary "reader" in the family, and this experience helped to prepare her for a teaching career.

Early Education

At the age of 15 Emma enrolled in a small "academy" in Worthington, Connecticut, about a mile from the family farm. She soon rose to the top of her class, helping younger children learn to read, memorize, and recite to the teacher. Within two years, at the age of 17, she became a teacher at the school during the summer term, and by the age of 19 had become the principal of the academy.

Principal of Middlebury Academy

After a short tenure in Worthington, the 20-year-old Emma took a position as principal of the prestigious Middlebury Academy in Vermont. The school, however, was more than 200 miles from her home, and this transition was difficult for the young woman.

Although Emma was happy that she had achieved a great deal in such a short time, she was disappointed with the curriculum at Middlebury. Like most female academies of this period, its primary curricular focus was to prepare young women for a life of middle-class domesticity. Though not necessarily opposed to teaching subjects such as sewing, cooking, flower arranging, and music, Emma had hoped to introduce more challenging academic subjects.

Dr. John Willard

Disillusioned and lonely, Emma continued at Middlebury for two years. Then at the age of 22, she met and married Dr. John Willard, 28 years her senior. She left her position at the school, moved into his large home, and helped raise his four children from a former marriage.

A New School

Despite her love for John, Emma was not satisfied with her life. She missed teaching and she missed her family. Her four stepchildren resented her, and

John was having some financial problems due to robbery at the bank of which he was the director. To help with the family's financial difficulties, Emma opened a small school in her home.

Collaboration

During this period, John's nephew moved in with the family while he was attending Middlebury College. Emma and John struck up a friendship and they often discussed the curriculum of the college. From these discussions she conceptualized a broader and more academically rigorous curriculum for her school. This was a turning point in her teaching career, and the collaboration of these two would change the trajectory of women's education for the rest of the nineteenth century and beyond.

Slowly Emma incorporated some of the courses offered at Middlebury College into her school. But despite these improvements in the curriculum, the school would not survive because of lack of funding. Emma spent as great deal of time attempting to secure a steady source of income for the school, but to no avail.

A Search for Funding

As a result of these disappointments, Emma Willard looked elsewhere for funding and chose New York State as a possible location for her school. The state had begun construction of the Erie Canal in 1817, and it had created an incredible economic boom in New York. Willard was determined to take advantage of this economic growth.

To encourage investment in her proposed school, she began to write *An Address to the Public: Particularly to the Members of the Legislature of New York Proposing a Plan for Improving Female Education.* Her idea was to present this *Plan* to the New York Legislature for funding a new school.

A Mixture of Traditional and New Ideas

But Willard understood the nature of the conservative male-dominated legislature of New York and fashioned her *Plan* to appeal to these policymakers. The *Plan* therefore emphasized the more traditional curricular dimensions of female education designed to train young women to become middle-class wives and mothers. Within the *Plan*, however, she also referenced academic subjects and preparation for teaching.

COMPONENTS OF THE PLAN

The *Plan* had three basic components. The first was the structure and organization of the seminary, the second was a comprehensive description of the curriculum, and the third centered on teacher training.

The *Plan* proposed that students would live at the seminary in small rooms that would accommodate two women. Common areas would be available for recitations, reading, and dance. In addition, these areas would also be equipped with maps, charts, and other materials for the study of science and geography. The seminary would have a library with books for instruction and free reading. It would also have musical instruments, a piano, and some paintings for art instruction.

The curriculum of the *Plan* had four parts: religion and moral instruction, literary instruction, domestic instruction, and ornamental branches. Each of these components was presented in detail.

Religion and Moral Instruction

Religion and moral Instruction was presented as the first component of the *Plan* of curriculum. Willard once again understood the generally conservative nature of the legislators that she wished to impress and, as a result, instruction was nonsectarian but Christian in focus.

Following church services on the Sabbath, for example, students would listen to "discourses relative to the particular duties of their sex." And then in the evenings, Willard herself would read from the Bible while students did their sewing.

In addition, each day Willard would emphasize to her students their important duties as wives and mothers. Finally, regarding dress, Emma always wore simple, modest black dresses with no adornments, as did all teachers. Her students were encouraged to do the same.

Literary Instruction

In terms of literary instruction, Emma emphasized the importance of reading with expression to interest their own children and young students if they became teachers. She also placed emphasis on the ability to simplify reading material so that their students and children could understand and appreciate it. In addition to literature, she also introduced more rigorous academic subjects such as science, geography, and philosophy.

Domestic Instruction

The third component of the curriculum was domestic instruction. Willard felt strongly that her charges should be able to attend to the duties of the household because it was essential for the comfort of their husbands and children. Students would practice their "housewifery" daily by cleaning and maintaining their rooms and making their beds.

Ornamental Branches and Grace of Motion

Willard also saw the "ornamental branches" of instruction as very important. This included drawing, painting, singing, playing an instrument, "elegant penmanship," needlework, and sewing, as well as mending and darning socks. She also felt strongly that women should develop grace of motion through dance. Each day, students would dance for an hour in the late morning. Dance, Emma noted, provided students with needed exercise, relaxation, and poise.

Laws and Regulations of the Seminary

Finally, in addition to the academic curriculum, Willard emphasized the importance of students understanding and obeying the "Laws and Regulations" of the seminary. Students should understand the organization and structure of life at the school, as well as the rules of behavior for students and instructors. Moreover, they should also be aware of the punishments "to be inflicted on offenders and the rewards . . . to be bestowed on the virtuous and diligent."

The *Plan* Goes Public

When Willard completed her draft of the *Plan* in 1819, two of her students sent a copy to a family friend, General van Schoonhoven, who was quite impressed. The general hand-delivered the *Plan* to Governor DeWitt Clinton of New York and Willard followed up with a personal letter to the governor introducing herself and enclosing a beautiful, hand-written copy of the *Plan* to him.

The Role of DeWitt Clinton

Clinton was a progressive for his time, and clearly was interested in education. As you will recall, he had supported Joseph Lancaster's monitorial schools and now was quite impressed with Emma Willard's plan for female education. He presented the plan to the New York State Legislature and requested a charter and funds to establish a seminary.

Lobbying in Albany

Emma and her husband John were jubilant, and traveled to Albany to personally lobby members of the legislature to support funding. Later, she wrote of this experience, "I had ... determined to go to the legislature and plead at the bar (with) my living voice; believing that I should throw forth my whole soul in the effort for my sex."

The Willards were delighted that the policymakers had granted them a charter for the school, but ultimately were disappointed that they balked at providing needed funding. Using logic that was typical of the day, legislators argued that by funding a school for women, money would be denied to men's institutions.

Positive Response

Willard, however, was not deterred for long and had her *Plan* published. She personally distributed copies of it to prominent men and political leaders throughout the nation. Among these were Thomas Jefferson, John Adams, and President James Monroe. Most of the responses were cordial, but John Adams's was both complimentary and clearly supportive of female education. Adams wrote Willard, noting: "Whenever I hear of a great man, I always inquire—Who was his mother."

Despite support and favorable responses from both prominent men and women through the country, funding for her seminary was not forthcoming. Once again, Willard was disappointed but resolved to move forward. Along with husband John, his grown children, and several of her best students, Emma moved to Waterford, New York, and used the charter granted for a school by the New York State Legislature to establish the Waterford Academy.

Waterford Academy: Surviving on a Shoestring

The Academy survived for three years on a shoestring budget derived primarily from John's work as a doctor and the meager tuition from the school. In desperation and on the brink of bankruptcy, in 1821 Emma received word from the Council of Troy, New York, that they had levied a special tax of $4,000 to support her school in their growing community.

A New Home in Troy

The Council purchased an abandoned three-story building in the heart of Troy for the school. The building, the former Moulton Coffee House, had 22 rooms and a large ballroom. A Board of Trustees for the school was appointed, as was a "Committee of Ladies" to work as a liaison between Emma and the Board. Emma Willard's dream was becoming a reality.

The entire Willard household, respected teachers, and Emma's best students packed their belongings, school supplies, and maps and set out for Troy, just five miles to the south. The extended "family" moved into temporary housing near the school.

Renovating the Seminary

During the summer of 1821, workers renovated the old coffee house with Willard personally supervising their work. She reported to the trustees that "I want you to make me a building that will suit my trade . . . and will not complain . . . provided you finish it so that we will not get slivers in our fingers due to rough boards."

The monumental collaborative task was completed by the beginning of the fall semester, 1821 and the school enrolled 90 students in grades 9 through 12. Students came from Massachusetts, Vermont, Connecticut, Ohio, South Carolina, Georgia, and New York.

Dr. John Willard's Important Role

Emma's husband, Dr. John Willard, played a key role in the early years of the Troy Female Seminary, handling all the finances of the school and serving as the primary physician for the young students. In addition, the fact that there was a doctor on call at the school certainly was a reassuring comfort to parents who were sending their young girls away to school. Tragically, John died just four years after the opening of the school.

New Subjects

The fall semester of 1821 was an exciting moment for female education in the new republic. Emma Willard's curricular plan was implemented with emphasis on domestic skills, academic subjects, and teacher training.

In addition to traditional subjects, Willard also was interested in teaching new subjects such as geography to expand the horizons of her students. But she felt the traditional methods of teaching this subject were inappropriate and abstract. Most geography texts available at the time, for example, began with maps of the world that had an "Anglocentric" perspective. Students typically were required to memorize distances from London to cities throughout the world.

Geography

As a result, Willard collaborated with William Channing Woodbridge, a noted geographer, to develop a new text. *The Woodbridge and Willard Geographies and Atlases*, published in 1823, provided a new focus on geography education. This book centered on the United States and began with an assignment for students to "draw a map of her hometown." For Willard, it was important for students to develop a sense of "place" to comprehend wider geographic areas.

Mathematics

Another subject that was often neglected in female education was mathematics. It was considered to be too complex for women. Years later, when Susan B. Anthony and her sisters were attending public school, their male teacher refused to teach them long division. He claimed that while addition and subtraction might be appropriate, long division was simply too difficult for young girls. An infuriated Anthony recalled this incident in her *Reminiscences*.

Willard intuitively understood this problem and resolved to teach math (and long division) to her charges. Her innovative techniques of instruction were derived in part from Pestalozzi, and she used everyday objects to demonstrate math concepts. In solid geometry, for example, she carved globes, cones, and pyramids from turnips and potatoes. Hand-cut paper triangles also were used to help students understand shapes in plain geometry.

History

In history education, Willard was once again disappointed with the books available for her students, especially with their typical "Anglo" focus. As a result, she wrote her own text entitled *A History of the United States or Republic of America* in 1828. This book was a patriotic work that placed special emphasis on the great figures in America's past and also provided students with an understanding of our political institutions.

In addition to her innovative approaches to various subjects, Willard integrated courses such as history, geography, and literature, once again anticipating modern methods of "whole language" instruction.

Teacher Education

A few of Willard's best students also were introduced to the teaching profession. Here they learned progressive techniques of discipline and instruction derived in part from John Locke and Jean-Jacques Rousseau. For example, future teachers were taught to avoid corporal punishment. Rather than correcting a misbehaving student in public, Willard suggested that they talk to the student in private. In short, physical violence and public humiliation of students in the classroom were virtually eliminated.

With regard to reading instruction, Emma emphasized comprehension rather than the traditional methods of memorization and recitation. In this way, she anticipated such important educational figures as Horace Mann, William McGuffey, and John Dewey.

COLLABORATION WITH FORMER STUDENTS

These new approaches soon distinguished Emma Willard as a leading educator. Her signature on a teaching certificate was said to be the "gold standard" of teaching excellence. Many of her students assumed teaching and administrative position in schools throughout the country. Their collaboration with Willard helped to transform the image of the female teacher in our culture and society.

Later, Willard founded the Willard Association for the Mutual Improvement of Female Teachers. As president of the organization, she promoted many of her progressive teaching methods and encouraged women to pursue higher education and self-improvement. Her collaborative efforts with her former students as well as other female teachers helped to establish women as a critical component of education, especially in the primary grades.

Julia Pierpoint

Willard was determined to promote ideas of both gender equity and female teaching through her collaboration with her many students. Julia Pierpoint, for example, was one of Emma's first students, and she helped establish the Troy Female Seminary. Pierpoint played an important role in the planning and development of the school and taught there during its early years.

Like many of the graduates of the Seminary, Pierpoint later took a position as a teacher. At the Female Academy in Sparta, Georgia, she taught hundreds of students. Later, she took a position as headmistress at what eventually became the South Carolina Female Collegiate Institute. There she directed the school's curriculum and, during a 12-year period, taught more than 4,000 students, many of whom became teachers themselves both in the South and in the West. Interestingly, one of Julia's prize students, Anna Maria Calhoun Clemson, with her husband Thomas Green Clemson, founded Clemson University.

Elizabeth Sherrill

When Julia Pierpont left Sparta, Elizabeth Sherrill, another of Emma's teacher graduates and assistants, took her place. Later Sherrill and her husband took charge of a female Academy in Augusta where she expanded the "Emma Willard network" for many years.

Urania Sheldon

Yet another of Emma's students, Urania Sheldon, established her own female academy in Washington County, New York, in 1825. Later she moved her school to Schenectady, New York, where she taught for several years. Eventually her reputation reached Utica, New York, and Sheldon was enlisted to come to this growing city and help establish the Utica Female Academy. In Utica she taught hundreds of students until 1842 when she married Eliphalet Nott, the president of Union College.

Caroline Livy

Caroline Livy, another graduate of Troy Female Seminary in 1841, went on to a distinguished career in teaching and also spread the ideas of Emma Willard. Upon her graduation, Livy and her husband traveled to Rome, Georgia, where she became the principal of a local female academy. During the next decade, the couple taught more than 5,000 young women, many of whom went on to careers in teaching.

Elmira Hart Lincoln Phelps

Emma Willard's younger sister, Elmira Hart Lincoln Phelps, also became an important figure in female education. After her studies at Troy, she taught at a number of district schools. She then traveled south to become the head of Patapsco Female Institute in Maryland. There she taught for many years employing the methods outlined by Willard in her famous *Plan*.

Elizabeth Cady Stanton

Although not a teacher in the conventional sense, one of Willard's most notable students was Elizabeth Cady Stanton. Stanton graduated from the Troy Seminary in 1832 and went on to a storied career advocating for the rights of women. In 1848, she and her fellow women activists launched the Seneca Falls Convention, the first major women's rights conference. Elizabeth wrote the famous *Declaration of the Rights and Sentiments* and, along with 68 women and 32 men, signed the famous and controversial document.

WILLARD'S INTERNATIONAL REPUTATION

During the final decades of her long life, Willard turned over the primary administrative and teaching responsibilities of the Troy Female Seminary to her sister, her daughters, and her son John and his two daughters. This gave her time to write, travel, and give lectures on the importance of female education.

In addition to her ongoing collaboration with her own students who often went on to distinguished teaching careers in the United States, Willard also developed an international reputation and collaborated with educators and important political figures throughout the world.

Willard and Lafayette

For example, Emma developed a personal and long-standing friendship with the Marquis de Lafayette, the famous Revolutionary War hero, during his tour of the United States in 1825. As a prominent figure both here and abroad, Lafayette helped to promote Willard's ideas on gender equity and the importance of female education throughout Europe.

When Emma traveled to Paris to meet with Lafayette and his three daughters, she was presented at the court of King Louis Philippe I. This, of course, gave Willard a certain gravitas as well as a platform to promote her ideas on the intellectual equality of women and their role in education.

During her subsequent travels to observe female schools throughout Europe, she expressed some disappointment but encouraged these schools to develop a more rigorous curriculum comparable to that of boys. As a quiet advocate of change, Willard made a deep impression on European educators for the next generation and beyond.

Growing Domestic Reputation

When Willard returned from Europe, she was invited to a convention of the County Superintendents of Common Schools of New York State to give an address. She agreed, but rather than speaking to the entire group, she gave her speech to a select group of 60 distinguished members (all men).

In her talk, Willard passionately mapped out the important role of women in the common schools and impressed all in attendance. The Syracuse address was a huge success and was published in newspapers and common school journals throughout the nation.

As a result of her success in Syracuse, Willard was asked to tour a number of counties in Southern New York to observe teachers' institutes. She began her tour in September 1845 traveling to Monticello, New York, in the Catskill mountains. There she taught 100 teachers, both men and women, in the new methods of instruction and on the role of women in the common schools. She also advocated for "career teachers" and argued enthusiastically that women were especially suited to teach young children.

In the next few weeks, Willard and one of her former students conducted similar institutes in Binghamton, Oswego, Cairo, and Rome, New York, traveling more than 700 miles and instructing more than 500 teachers.

National Tour

Fresh from her success in New York, Willard was persuaded to make a similar tour throughout the southern and western states. She agreed, and in the next year Willard traveled more than 8,000 miles with her niece, Jenny Lincoln, visiting nearly all the major cities in every state west and south of New York.

The intrepid duo traveled by stagecoach, packet, canal boat, and private carriage. At every stop she was greeted enthusiastically by her "daughters" whom she had taught at Troy and went on to establish their own schools, institutes, and female academies. This collaboration spread the ideas of female education to the far corners of nineteenth-century America.

Later Life

In the final years of her life, Willard retired to her beloved Troy Seminary. Willard lived in a small red brick cottage on the school's property that was built especially for her, and she was often seen strolling through the campus. Occasionally on Sundays, she invited the highest performing students of each class to her home for tea and intellectual discussion. Willard died quietly in her cottage on April 15, 1870, surrounded by her students and teachers. All understood that an icon of education had passed from the earth.

Gender equity in both the field of education and in society was launched by this modest woman who believed in the intellectual equality of women and men. Although Emma Willard was not considered a "feminist" in the strict sense of the word, her vision of equity would propel women toward equality in the classrooms of the nation. Her collaborative work promoting teacher education and her relentless emphasis on the ideal of the intellectual equality of men and women helped to transform the world of education.

Chapter 5

The Common School

As we have seen, the late eighteenth to the early nineteenth centuries were a crucial period in the history of American education. Powerful figures on both sides of the Atlantic promoted new progressive ideas of reform that often included education. The European Enlightenment of the eighteenth century produced figures such as John Locke, Jean-Jacques Rousseau, and Voltaire, each of whom provided new approaches to curriculum, discipline, and inclusion as well as the movement toward secular education and the child-centered approach to learning.

EARLY EDUCATIONAL REFORM

This period also witnessed the American Revolution, which not only launched the worldwide democratic revolutions of this era, but also helped to transform our ideas regarding education. The idealistic visions and collaboration of figures such as Benjamin Franklin, Thomas Jefferson, and Benjamin Rush were stillborn, however, because of the Tenth Amendment to the U.S. Constitution that gave individual states total control of educational policy.

By the early nineteenth century, individuals such as Joseph Lancaster and his collaboration with the Quaker community brought attention to the plight of both enslaved Africans as well as the children of the new poor in both England and the United States. This collaboration also helped to create new approaches to learning and reinforced more humane forms of discipline in the classroom.

Emma Willard, on the other hand, championed the idea of intellectual equality of men and women and was a fierce advocate for her Troy Female Seminary and other schools for women. In addition, she promoted the idea of women teachers in the United States and, as a result of her collaboration with students and followers, was able to transform our ideas regarding education in America.

Figure 5.1. Horace Mann, father of the common school, ca. 1849. Drawing, unknown author.   https://commons.wikimedia.org/w/index.php?search=horace+mann&title=Special:MediaSearch&go=Go&type=image.

And yet, by the mid-1830s, the United States still struggled to embrace a universal system of education. Most states simply ignored the need for public schools, instead deferring to traditional private schools, tutors, and the occasional charity school.

MARKET REVOLUTION

Nevertheless, things were beginning to change. America's first Industrial Revolution in the 1820s had begun to transform our collective ideas regarding the need for education and spawned a collaboration among numerous groups and individuals. Moreover, a growing number of secular and religious reformers, commercial farmers, workingmen organizations, and small business owners began to call for some form of public education.

CHANGING DEMOGRAPHICS

Reformers also recognized the changing demographics of the nation as thousands of immigrants came to American shores looking for freedom and educational opportunities for their children. They argued that only through a common school education would these new Americans be able to assimilate into our culture and begin to appreciate our democratic values.

GRASSROOTS SUPPORT

On the other hand, both commercial farmers and members of workingmen's organizations understood that in this new meritocratic economy, only through free access to education could their children achieve a piece of the American Dream. Their collaborative support of the common school was critical.

Finally, small business owners recognized the utility of improved education. Workers who had a basic primary education were better workers, they were more punctual, and they had the skills of reading, writing, and arithmetic that would help them perform well in the workplace.

Political parties were slow to heed these changes at both the local and national level, but eventually responded to the growing call for a new direction in education. While both the Democratic and the Whig parties managed to garner some support for change, the Whigs took the lead.

HORACE MANN

In Massachusetts, the birthplace of Puritan schools during the seventeenth century, there was some support for public education but, like other states throughout the nation, the question of finance loomed large. By the mid-1830s, however, the Whig party of Massachusetts was able to push through a very modest proposal to create a State Board of Education. Then, in a rather astounding move, they selected a relatively unknown political figure—Horace Mann—as secretary of that body.

Horace Mann was not an educator and had never set foot in the classroom either as a teacher or as an administrator. But he was part of a reform juggernaut that was sweeping across the nation. Mann embraced a variety of social, political, and economic reforms including women's rights, abolition, Native American rights, national bankruptcy legislation, temperance, the humane treatment of the mentally ill and, eventually, the common school.

THE WHIG PARTY

The Whig Party of the 1830s was a relatively new political entity. It had emerged in opposition to the policies of the powerful Democratic Party led by Andrew Jackson, Martin Van Buren, and others. Under Jackson, Democrats had embraced a states' rights policy platform that insisted that schools continue to be controlled by the states, with no federal support or direction.

Whigs, on the other hand, argued that the federal, state, and local governments had an important responsibility in the development of the nation as a whole. As a result, they promoted "internal improvements," a strong national banking system, tariffs to protect American industries, a more centralized social agenda to improve the lives of Americans and, eventually the common school.

HORACE MANN AND THE COMMON SCHOOL

It was this changing political environment, fueled by the collaboration of diverse reform elements, that provided a unique opportunity for the development of the common school. In 1836, along with several of his Whig colleagues, including James Carter, Mann lobbied for state funds to support the handful of schools scattered throughout the state. This request, however, was blocked by the legislature.

The following year, however, Mann's collaboration within the Whig caucus pushed for the creation of a State Board of Education. The purpose of the board was modest. Its function was simply to collect information on the state of education in Massachusetts. The measure passed and was signed into law by the governor. To his astonishment, Mann was selected as secretary over Carter, who had been a leading advocate of education for his entire career.

At first, Mann hesitated to accept this position. He was apprehensive that his lack of experience in education might upend the fragile common school reform movement. He also felt strongly that James Carter, the great educator, deserved this position. But finally he agreed to take the job and began to prepare himself for this monumental task.

Preparing for His New Position

Mann immersed himself in the literature on schools and education. He studied the centralized Prussian educational system and the schools in Great Britain and France. He visited schools throughout Massachusetts and was absolutely appalled with their condition. He met with educators throughout the state; collaborated with Whig politicians, and consulted with the general public to develop his ideas regarding the common school.

Two Diverse Roles

Through this extensive consultation and collaboration, Mann eventually developed a plan to create schools throughout the state that would be academically sound and promote a common culture for a diverse student population. In addition, Mann understood that he also had to convince those with "school support hesitancy" of the need for public education.

In both areas, he was successful. Through his collaborative work with others in the state, he promoted the idea of a public school system that would provide students with the fundamentals of education and a common culture.

Common School Journal

And through his important essays in his *Common School Journal*, Mann articulated a philosophy of the absolute right of education for all Americans. He also made convincing arguments regarding the economic, political, and social benefits of common schools. Finally, with his collaborators within the field of education, he helped to create normal schools throughout the state to train teachers for the future.

The collaboration of Horace Mann and the Whigs of the mid-nineteenth century transformed the nation. Their work convinced educational reformers in other states, such as Henry Barnard and Calvin Wiley, to embrace the idea of universal education. The nation would not be the same!

WHO WAS HORACE MANN?

But who was Horace Mann? Like many of the reformers of this period, Horace came from very humble beginnings. He was not a "born leader." In fact, he grew up in a very poor farming family in Franklin, Massachusetts, where his brothers and sisters helped the family survive. There was little time for their education.

Loss of Father and Brother

Rather, Horace's father taught his sons how to read and write while his mother trained his sisters to cook, clean, and tend to the kitchen garden. Tragically, Horace's father died of tuberculosis when Horace was not yet 14 years old. Then the following year, his older brother Steven drowned in a local pond while fishing. Losing both his father and the brother whom he looked to for advice and counsel had a profound impact on Horace. When his other brother, Stanley, left home to manage a local textile mill, Horace was left to tend to the family farm.

Mann's Dream of Education

But Mann was no farmer. He understood that farming was an admirable profession, but he personally perceived life as a yeoman as little more than back-breaking work. He saw other boys in his community pack up and "go to college," and he dreamed of attending Brown University, just 30 miles to the south of his boyhood home.

Once Mann made the decision to leave farming and attend Brown, he began studying for his entrance examinations. The focus of his study was Latin, Greek, and mathematics. He read on his own and was a frequent visitor to the local Franklin Library. Later, he was tutored by two pastors in town who had helped other boys prepare for their exams. After nearly two years of study he finally felt that he was ready.

In 1816, Mann left home and traveled to Brown in Providence, Rhode Island, where he had arranged to take his oral entrance exams. He later recalled the excitement and fear that gripped him as he arrived on campus and approached President Asa Messer's office.

SHOULD I STAY OR SHOULD I GO?

As young Horace waited for the president to arrive, he was gripped with self-doubt. After all, he had never set foot in a classroom in his entire life. His knowledge was derived from independent study and a bit of tutoring. Was this enough? Should he simply slip out of the office and return home? "Should I stay or should I go?"

Mann Passes His Exams

But before he was able to decide, President Messer entered his office and immediately required Mann to translate several passages from the Greek Testament, a commonly used fourth-century version of the New Testament of the Bible. Horace struggled, but was able to complete the translation as President Messer looked on. Then on cue, professors Calvin Park and Jasper Adams entered the chamber and required him to translate passages from Virgil.

Once again, Horace struggled a bit but completed the task. He was then asked to wait in the adjoining room for their decision. After what must have seemed to be an eternity, the three professors, led by President Messer, informed him that while he had some "deficiencies," he had passed his exams and was admitted as a sophomore.

Graduation and Beyond

Mann was ecstatic and plunged into his studies with vigor and purpose. His hard work paid off and in three years he graduated from Brown with honors. His address to the graduating class was entitled "The Progressive Character of the Human Race," and foretold Horace's future direction as an activist, lawyer, legislator, and educator.

After graduation, Mann did some tutoring and worked as a librarian at Brown University, managing to take courses at Litchfield Law School at the same time. He graduated from Litchfield and was admitted to the bar in 1823. He then practiced as an attorney and became active in the growing reform movements of this period. Mann was profoundly interested in promoting the humane treatment of the mentally ill and eventually helped establish an asylum in Worcester, Massachusetts.

Mann Enters Politics

His activism and passion for reform propelled him into politics, and, in 1827, at the age of 31, he was elected to the Massachusetts state legislature. For the next eight years, Mann climbed the governmental ladder within the Whig caucus.

During these years Mann also continued his reform efforts. In addition, he spent several months in the summer of 1835 revising the Massachusetts state statutes, providing detailed marginal notes to assist with judicial review. This monumental task did not go unnoticed, and soon he was seen by the Whig leadership as a rising star. In fact, on completion of his task he was cited by the committee for "faithful, laborious and dignified discharge of . . . duties."

JAMES CARTER: THE FORGOTTEN MAN

It was at this point that Mann began his important collaboration with James Gordon Carter, the noted educator, in their common quest for educational reform in Massachusetts. Carter is the forgotten man in this story. He had a profound impact on the thinking of Mann, but his own career came to an abrupt end when he was passed over for the position of secretary of the Massachusetts Board of Education.

James Carter was born in Leominster, Massachusetts, in September 1775. About 20 years Mann's senior, Carter had been a tireless reformer, especially in the area of education. Like Mann, Carter came from humble beginnings and was raised on a small hardscrabble farm with his 12 brothers and sisters.

Carter's Early Life

As the oldest son of this large family group, James Carter was expected to take over the operation of the farm when he reached maturity. But like his younger colleague, Carter had a different future in mind. He wanted to go to college. To achieve that goal, he taught in the winter terms at a local district school and saved his money for tuition.

By the age of 18 Carter had saved enough to enroll at Groton Academy (now Lawrence Academy). Here he would begin his preparation for Harvard. And like many others at this time, Carter would attend Groton during the regular term and then teach at district schools during the winter terms.

Harvard

By the age of 21, Carter had completed his classical studies at Groton and saved enough money to pay his tuition. He spent the next three years at Harvard and excelled in his studies. By the end of his junior year, he was widely seen by his professors and fellow students as "apt to teach," and his career as an educator began in earnest.

Carter then took a difficult assignment, teaching a class of seamen from the "China trade" who were determined to improve their lives through education. Though challenging, Carter was successful and received thanks from both his students and the town leaders at the end of the term.

Collaboration with Warren Colburn

In 1820, Carter graduated from Harvard near the top of his class. He and his classmate Warren Colburn soon developed a friendship based in part on their common interest in education. Colburn would write *First Lessons in Arithmetic on the Plan of Pestalozzi* in 1821 and revolutionize the study of arithmetic for children. His approach to education in general would provide an important intellectual foundation for James Carter.

Following graduation, Carter moved to Lancaster, Massachusetts, where he became a tutor to wealthy young men who were preparing for college. Later, he would establish a private school for problem adolescents. Carter would retain his connection with the school throughout much of his life.

Abysmal District Schools

During this period, Carter began to understand that the quality of district school education was abysmal and had "moral and intellectual deficiencies." He was determined to transform these schools and to help create an improved common school experience for the children of Massachusetts and beyond.

Mrs. Richard Cleveland

Carter's new ideas caught the attention of a prominent member of Lancaster society by the name of Mrs. Richard Cleveland. Mrs. Cleveland, wife of a Salem sea captain and an intellectual in her own right, had studied the writings of both Pestalozzi and Rousseau. Later, she established a "symposium" on education in her home.

Cleveland's Symposium

Mrs. Cleveland invited local intellectuals including historian Jared Sparks; George Barrell Emerson, a pioneer in women's education; Elizabeth Peabody, founder of the first English-language kindergarten in the United States; as well as Warren Colburn. Carter was invited into this group and developed his educational reform ideas through his collaboration with other members of Cleveland's symposium.

Carter's Political Ascendancy

Through his connections with this group, James Carter became a favorite among the progressive leaders of Lancaster as an outspoken advocate for the Whig Party. In addition, he was drawn into the growing reform movements that advocated for women's rights, temperance, abolitionism, and education.

Letters

In 1821, James Carter began a series of articles in the *Boston Transcript* that launched his career as an educational reformer. The articles were collected and published as a pamphlet in 1824, entitled *Letters to the Honorable William Prescott on the Free Schools of New England with Remarks upon the Principles of Instruction*.

In his *Letters*, Carter discussed the rise and fall of educational ideas in the United States, from the idealistic visions of founding fathers through the early national period that witnessed a sharp decline in public support for education at the state level. From his own experiences in the classroom, he also described the sorry state of grammar school education in both the winter and summer school terms.

Recommended Changes in Education

Carter went on to advocate for changes in the organization, administration, and especially the financing of district schools. He argued that the state had sufficient funds to improve these schools, but that support for grammar schools had been ignored. Only through a vigorous funding system, he wrote, could these problems be solved.

Carter's *Letters* also revealed an important reform impulse. The changes that he advocated would help to equalize opportunities and prevent the dominance of the few over the many. Moreover, it would help to preserve free institutions in both politics and society.

The Two Great Defects of District Schools

Carter went on to note that there were two great defects in the district schools: poor teachers and bad textbooks. Teacher training was essential. He argued that "education was a science and instruction was an art" and, therefore, teachers should be taught in advanced schools designed specifically for teacher education.

Carter also wrote that the textbooks that were available at the time were misdirected. He felt that they violated Locke's doctrine of mental development in that they focused on memorization and abstractions. Rather, he advocated for textbooks that began with common experiences and then moved toward generalizations. This "Pestalozzian" approach was central to Carters' method of teaching.

Reform Essays of 1825

Following the success of his *Letters*, Carter wrote a series of essays for the *Boston Patriot* and *Mercantile Advisor*. These articles, published in 1825, expanded on his *Letters* and demanded reforms in education.

Central to Carter's argument was his idea that education was essential to society and therefore was the responsibility of all citizens. For Carter, schools must prepare students to "discharge all the duties that society requires." In short, Carter argued that schools should not only teach children the basics, but socialize them as well.

"Thistle in the Vineyard of the Republic"

Additionally, Carter noted that in a democratic republic, it was the responsibility of the school and society to produce enlightened students who would maintain our form of government and society. He went on to note that parsimonious taxpayers and legislators had neglected the public schools and had placed our government in danger. They represented the "thistle in the vineyard of the republic."

Essays upon Popular Education

Carter's ideas, drawn from his essays in the *Boston Patriot*, were published as a pamphlet in 1826 as *Essays upon Popular Education or Influence of an Early Education*. This pamphlet, although controversial, brought attention to the plight of public schools in Massachusetts and led to Carter's growing national and international reputation as an important educational reformer.

As a result of Carter's work and the accolades he received from distinguished journalists throughout the northeast, Massachusetts passed a series of laws that both established and provided support for the first public high school in 1827. In addition, the Massachusetts State School Fund was established in 1834. This fund provided modest financial support for public grammar schools.

Collaboration with Horace Mann

In 1834, Carter was elected to the Massachusetts House of Representatives, where he served for three terms and was a member of the House Committee on Education. Then, in 1837, he was elected to the Massachusetts State Senate. It was during this period that his collaboration with Horace Mann began. Both he and Mann were powerful advocates of the common school:

Carter with his intellectual reform approach to education, and Mann with his political acumen and leadership.

State Board of Education

Earlier, in 1836, Horace Mann and a handful of his Whig colleagues had advocated for funding of common schools but were unsuccessful. Then, in 1837, when James Carter became a member of the Senate, their critical collaboration led to the establishment of the State Board of Education of Massachusetts.

Once again, it was the collaboration of these two men and a group of Whig reformers that made it possible to push this important piece of legislation through the Senate. Mann's leadership as the presiding officer of this body and Carter's gravitas and intellectual power provided the momentum for success.

When the bill was signed into law, Governor Everett of Massachusetts appointed a group of eight distinguished men to serve on the board. James Carter was chosen as its first member. Horace Mann was also appointed to the board largely through the support of Edmund Dwight, an influential merchant from Boston. The board's initial charge was to select a secretary who would lead the group.

HORACE MANN BECOMES SECRETARY

To the surprise of nearly everyone, the board voted for Horace Mann as secretary. While Mann had little practical background in education, he was seen as the likely choice because he had legal training and political skills. On the other hand, while James Carter was a well-known educational reformer, his positions often were seen as too radical, and he had little political experience.

As we have seen, while Horace was honored by the board's action, he hesitated to accept this new position. His political career was on the rise, and many felt that he would soon run for governor of the state. Horace also felt that he was ill equipped to become the secretary of this board. Certainly, his colleague James Carter was much more qualified than he.

For more than a week, Mann grappled with this decision to the point where he was unable to work. He wrote in his journal: "Count that day lost, whose low, declining sun, views from thy hand, no worthy action done." Finally, at the last minute, Mann informed the committee that he would accept this position.

Preparation for the Challenge Ahead

Horace Mann took the challenge seriously. He traveled throughout Massachusetts and visited district schools across the state. He immersed himself in the educational literature available to him, including the writings of James Simpson, the famous British advocate of public education, and Victor Cousin's *Report on the Prussian School System*. Mann also pored through back issues of the *Journal of Education* and the *North American Review*. And he paid special attention to James Carter's numerous essays and pamphlets.

In addition to his general reading on education, Mann examined numerous town reports on the condition of schools. It was here that he recognized their pathetic state. In Westport, Massachusetts, for example, one teacher reported that she taught 15 students in a cramped 14-by-16-foot room. Other teachers complained that they had no outhouses, and one wrote that their school had "bare walls—no maps—no other apparatus, save the switch or ferule."

An Intellectual Turning Point

As Horace prepared to assume his position as secretary, he attended a lecture that would have a profound impact on him and his direction in education. The lecture, delivered by Ralph Waldo Emerson, was entitled "The American Scholar." It was an address delivered at Cambridge to the Harvard chapter of the Phi Beta Kappa society.

Emerson encouraged Americans to step up to their rightful place in the world. He noted that our long "apprenticeship to the learning of other lands" had come to an end. The American moment had arrived. The world of tomorrow, Emerson noted, would not be led by the old order but by the common man.

And then came a statement that certainly had an impact on Mann as well as others in attendance. Emerson declared in direct prose: "I ask not for the great, the remote, the romantic . . . I embrace the common, I explore and sit at the feet of the familiar, the low."

Horace Mann, still in his 30s, was profoundly moved by Emerson's words and, coming at a time when he was just embarking a new career path, they would shape the direction of his work. He wrote that this new direction would help to create "a new form of education for Americans, one that would reach the rich and the poor alike and . . . promote a common educational experience."

Collaboration with Transcendentalists

In addition to Mann's preparations for his new position, he also began an important collaboration with the New England Transcendentalists. Central to this networking was Elizabeth Peabody. Just a few years before his appointment as secretary of the Board of Education, Mann met Elizabeth and Mary Peabody at their common boarding house in Boston.

Horace was recently widowed, and the two women supported him both emotionally and intellectually. Both Peabody sisters were well educated and taught at Amos Bronston Alcott's Temple School in Boston.

The Transcendental Club

In 1840, Elizabeth Peabody opened a bookstore and lending library in Boston that became the meeting place for the Transcendental Club. Mann frequently attended meetings of the club, and gradually he and Mary Peabody become very good friends. In fact, Mary became his assistant during Horace's early years as secretary of the Board of Education. The two married in 1843.

Throughout these years Horace, Mary, Elizabeth, Sophia Peabody and her husband Nathanial Hawthorne, Ralph Waldo Emerson, William Ellery Channing, and the entire Transcendental Club often discussed the reforms of the day, including education. It was through these collaborations that Horace Mann further developed his understanding of the needs of education and the importance of the common school.

MARY PEABODY MANN

Mann's collaboration with the Transcendentalists clearly had an important impact on his development. Perhaps equally as important was his partnership with his wife Mary, who remained his secretary, confidant, and supporter for the rest of his life. Their rather unconventional "honeymoon" in 1843, for example, actually was a working holiday in Europe. The two visited schools in England, Scotland, and Holland, but they were especially interested in the centralized educational system in Prussia.

Prussian System of Education

The Prussian system of education was the innovation of Frederick the Great in the late 1700s. Frederick understood the importance of education, especially in a nation like Prussia that was immersed in poverty and in the throes of an ancient medieval culture. As a result, he instituted a number of important reforms including the *general landschulreglement* decree in 1763. This led to the creation of a new school system in Prussia.

The decree created a centralized educational ladder that required all boys and girls to be educated in state-run schools. The system began with compulsory *Volkschule* that called for eight years of primary education for all Prussian children.

The *Realschule*, Prussia's secondary schools, followed and expanded the curriculum and introduced students to a language other than German. Brighter students then went on to the *Gymnasium* to prepare for university study, while others did an apprenticeship to learn a trade.

Horace and Mary Mann were astounded with this system. They liked the fact that schools were tax supported, that education was compulsory, and that there was a clear educational ladder leading to a career. They also were delighted that there was an emphasis on professional teacher training in normal schools. Finally, the newlyweds were impressed with Prussia's rigorous assessment of students' educational progress and a common curriculum for each grade level.

Fundamental Propositions

When Horace and Mary Mann returned from their European tour, they now had a more complete vision of the nature of educational reform. Together they developed a number of "fundamental propositions."

The most important of these was the need for public education to maintain a virtuous democracy. In this context, Horace Mann wrote that public education must be supported financially by the people and through cooperation with teachers and school administrators.

The Pragmatic Need for Education

The Manns' second proposition was pragmatic and reminiscent of Benjamin Rush. It focused on the need to provide education to those who might turn to crime if they did not have the means to support themselves. The state would save the costs to build and support jails and prisons. Mann also pointed out that public education was essential for the development of the modern economy. Schools provided disciplinary habits and basic reading and writing skills that were necessary for industrial and mercantile occupations.

Diversity and Inclusion

Mann's third proposition was that education was essential to socializing the diverse immigrant groups that were settling in the state and the nation. A common school experience, he argued, would promote patriotism and encourage greater acceptance of diverse cultures and religions among all students.

Secular Education

The fourth proposition focused on the importance of secular education and the separation of school and religion. Like Rousseau, Lancaster, and others before him, Mann felt that while moral teaching was important, it should be presented in a nonsectarian manner that would promote a nationalistic, pan-Protestant vision of America. This would help students understand their responsibilities to God and country.

New Techniques of Discipline

Mann's fifth principle was the rejection of corporal punishment. Here Mann was informed by his intellectual collaboration with Locke and especially Rousseau. As we have seen, Rousseau recognized the basic goodness of children who were corrupted by society. For these foundationalists, the use of corporal punishment on children was therefore counterproductive.

The use of the ferule, switch, and whipping post of course had been the favorite tool of discipline for centuries and was supported by biblical tradition. Mann rejected those methods, however, and like Lancaster before him, he favored psychological rather than physical punishment in both the classroom and at home.

Pedagogy of Love

Mann's sixth proposition was related to his ideas on discipline. He argued that women were better suited than men to promote what he called the "pedagogy of love." His collaboration with Mary Mann, Elizabeth Peabody, the Transcendentalists, as well as Emma Willard certainly had an impact on this important idea. Later, Alonzo Potter, the great pedagogue who also supported this idea, wrote that women "were preeminently qualified to administer . . . a moral influence on children."

Teacher Training

Mann's final proposition centered on the importance of teacher training in normal schools. He argued throughout his career that teachers must be trained in subject matter, pedagogy, curriculum, and disciplinary techniques. Unlike Lancaster, who used untrained monitors as teachers, Mann favored specialized preparation in normal schools. During his tenure as secretary of the Board of Education, Mann helped to establish three such schools in the state.

While Massachusetts was not quite ready for many of these innovations, the Manns saw state control of education and public funding of schools as essential to its development. Prussia had provided them with a model of educational development and demonstrated how it could transform a nation socially, economically, and politically.

Common School Journal

Horace Mann had a powerful voice in promoting the common school in his state. He did so with his bully pulpit and his tireless advocacy for education among his colleagues in the legislature. In addition, his *Common School Journal* and his 12 annual reports informed the state and the nation of the progress of educational reform.

U.S. Congressman

After 12 years as secretary of the Board of Education of Massachusetts, Mann was recruited by friends and colleagues to replace U.S. Congressman John Quincy Adams, who had died that year. Though hesitant, Mann finally accepted the position and became a strong reform advocate for the next several years in Congress, working with the Whig Party and his friend and colleague, Daniel Webster.

But these were tumultuous times, and the fate of the nation seemed to hang on the question of both the morality and the expansion of slavery in the nation. Mann had a middle-of-the-road position on these questions. On the one hand, he was a strong opponent of slavery on moral grounds, but had not aligned with "radical" Whig abolitionists such as Wendell Phillips and William Lloyd Garrison.

Mann Breaks with His Party

But his major break from politics came when he refused to align himself with Daniel Webster. In his now infamous "Seventh of March Speech," Webster proposed a compromise with Democrats on the issue of slavery, concerned deeply about the possibility of civil conflict regarding this issue.

When Mann refused to endorse this compromise, he appeared to have turned his back on both Webster and the Whig Party. As a result, Mann became a pariah, and his political career as a Whig—at least—was over. Later he was courted by the Free Soil Party to run for governor of Massachusetts, but he decided to remain outside of politics.

Antioch College

At about the same time, in 1852, he was asked to become the president of the newly established, progressive, nonsectarian, biracial, and coeducational Antioch College. Mann accepted the position, and in the next few years of financial struggle and eventual bankruptcy, he led the school to success both academically and fiscally.

The great educator and "father of the common school" had now brought his skills and passions to a new level at Antioch College. When he passed from this world in 1859, surrounded by his family and students, each recognized that education in this country had been transformed by this unassuming man and his collaborators.

In one of Mann's most cogent addresses to the college, he summarized his legacy on education, stating: "Be ashamed to die until you have won some victory for humanity." For Horace Mann, that victory was the common school.

Chapter 6

A Curriculum for the Nation

The networking and collaboration of reform-minded Americans had become a powerful force by the 1830s. A new generation—born around the turn of the nineteenth century, following the tumult of the American Revolution and

Figure 6.1. *McGuffey's Eclectic Primer*, ca. 1909. https://commons.wikimedia.org/wiki/File:McGuffey%27s_eclectic_primer_(1909)_(14730215426).jpg.

constitutional periods—had begun to address a wide array of political, social, economic, and educational issues.

POLITICAL, SOCIAL, AND ECONOMIC REFORM

Politically, states were extending the franchise, and increasingly more Americans were now able to participate in the electoral process. While women, African Americans, and many others still did not have the vote, historians have referred to this period as the "era of the common man" because voter participation soared and a wave of political reforms swept through the nation.

Social activists also turned their attention to women's rights, the plight of enslaved Africans, the poor, the mentally ill, immigrants and, for a few, Native Americans. One the driving forces of this new expression of reform emerged from the explosion of religiosity, what historians call the "Second Great Awakening." This new movement embraced a more personal religious experience and encouraged new empathetic attitudes toward the less fortunate.

Economically, the nation was fresh from what economists have called the "first Industrial Revolution." This in turn had strengthened the country fiscally and fostered both an increase in the disposable income of Americans as well as the onset of the market revolution. These changes promoted consumerism and materialism, and helped to expand the economy even further.

EDUCATIONAL REFORM

As these fundamental changes in American life were unfolding, a new sensibility regarding education also was emerging. Political, social, and economic reforms dovetailed with the call for the common school.

Democrats in major cities and Whigs throughout the north had begun to appreciate the importance of a common school education for their constituents. Slowly states began to abandon their age-old opposition to public schools. Then, too, workingmen organizations fought for free schools, recognizing that only through education would their children be able to enjoy the "American Dream."

Small businessmen also saw the benefits of public education in creating a quality workforce, and the new commercial farmers of this era saw public education for their children as the key to their future and a stronger, more developed nation. The movement collaboration of these disparate groups was a powerful force that helped educational crusaders realize school reforms and eventually create the common school.

SLOW CHANGE

And yet, change was slow. When Horace Mann observed schools in Massachusetts in the late 1830s, he was appalled by their lack of basic educational materials for students. As we have seen, some schools had no outhouses, no blackboards, no slates, but often were well equipped with hard roughhewn benches and plenty of switches and ferules for punishment.

BOOKS

And then there was the pathetic lack of books in schools. Some students had to share a book that they brought from home; others might borrow a book from the teacher, and still others would read from the well-worn family Bible. Even in the wealthier communities of New England and along the mid-Atlantic coast, there were few standardized readers except for a version of *The New England Primer*, hopelessly out of date even by the standards of the 1830s.

The New England Primer

The New England Primer had been reshaped throughout the years and was used in a number of early nineteenth-century American communities. But the basic form and content of these *Primers* remained nearly identical to the earlier volumes first published in the late seventeenth century.

The Primer was centered on basic Puritan beliefs derived from the Bible. The pedagogy focused on rote memorization of prayers and biblical verses. These *Primers* also embraced the biblical vision of the essential depravity of children and centered on the absolute authority of both parents and God.

The New England Primer was originally a book of prayers and devotions and included the Lord's Prayer, the Ten Commandments, and a selection of scriptures. As *The Primer* developed throughout the years, the biblical scriptures were often reduced to simple axioms that could be understood by young children.

The Primer typically included an annotated alphabet, vowel and consonant sounds, and "easie syllables for children." The latter included a total of 140 total combinations that children were expected to memorize. These were followed in order by words of one, two, three, and then four syllables.

Annotated Alphabet

The alphabet, on the other hand, included the famous 24 woodcuts with accompanying rhymes. These simple rhyming verses provided children with lessons on how to live their lives and were often expressions drawn from the Bible. For example, for the letter "A," children read: "In Adams fall we sinned all." For the letter "F," we see an emphasis on a productive and busy child, with the fear of corporal punishment clearly presented: "The idle fool is whipt at school."

Catechism

In addition to syllables and the annotated alphabet, *The Primer* contained the "Shorter Catechism" consisting of questions and answers focused on the Puritan's interpretation of religion. These were to be memorized by students. One example is, "Question: What is God? Answer: God is a spirit, infinite, eternal and unchangeable in His being, wisdom, power, holiness, justice, goodness and truth."

Memorization

The primary method of teaching reading was also proscribed in *The Primer*. It involved a four-stage memorization process. First, students memorized the alphabet with all its religious references. They proceeded to memorize letters and consonant combinations, then moved on to memorize phonetic sounds as part of their "easie syllables." Finally, children proceeded to memorize short passages derived from the Bible itself.

Learning (primarily memorization) was acquired individually on the hard benches of the schoolhouse and when called upon, students were required to recite the material to the teacher. Comprehension was not a priority, and only later would students interpret and understand the material that they read.

In the wake of the American Revolution and constitutional period, a few new textbooks emerged that were a bit more secular in nature and expressed in part the values of the new republic. The most important of these was Noah Webster's *American Spelling Book*. This book, often referred to as *The Blue Back Speller*, became the standard text for academies and private schools during the late eighteenth and early nineteenth centuries.

The Blue Back Speller

Unlike *The New England Primer*, *The Blue Back Speller* was arranged to help students progress by age from simple material to more complex passages. The

Speller, moreover, was secular in nature and there was no mention of God, the Bible, or scriptures. Rather, Webster included a number of important events in American history beginning with the "discovery of America" by Columbus in 1492 and the battle of Yorktown in 1781.

The Blue Back Speller was an important step in the development of the reading curriculum for American children, but it was not widely adopted. And by the early 1830s the books were considered outdated. It was in this environment that William McGuffey published his first series of *Readers* that would revolutionize reading instruction for the emerging common schools.

COLLABORATION

While William Holmes McGuffey penned these famous *Readers* and helped to transform public education in the process, he was not alone. His ideas and approaches to education were informed by a host of collaborators that would shape the common school movement of this era.

MCGUFFEY: EARLY LIFE AND EDUCATION

McGuffey, or "old Guff" as he was affectionately known later in life, was born in Claysville, Pennsylvania, at the turn of the nineteenth century. While he was still a young child, the family moved to the Ohio frontier, and William grew up in poverty on their small hardscrabble farm.

His mother, Anna, recognized that William was a precocious child and began reading to him daily. She also traced letters and figures in the ashes in the fireplace so that William could learn to read and count. Anna was successful, and William became a bit of a prodigy. When he entered school, for example, it was clear that he was too advanced, and he left after just a few months.

A Path through the Woods

The family then decided that William should attend Reverend Wick's school in Youngstown, Ohio, six miles from their farm. The problem, however, was that there was no road between the two towns. William's father, Sandy, and his grandfather were determined that he attend Wick's school, and in the next few months, they cleared a path through the woods so that William and his sister could go to school.

When the path was completed, William and his sister set out for the school's winter term and stayed with the good reverend during the week. On weekends the two young children would make the six-mile trek back to their Coitsville home.

Early Teaching

Then, at the tender age of 14, William became a teacher himself. He taught in a subscription school in Calcutta, Ohio, about 60 miles from his home. His goal was to make enough money so that he could continue his education. William taught in Calcutta for four years but the long hours, the lack of support from the community, the poor quality of students, and the isolation from his family finally led him to close the school.

At the age of 18, McGuffey was recruited by Reverend Thomas Hughes to attend the Greersburg Academy in Darlington, Pennsylvania. He was a good student and he lived in Reverend Hughes's home, doing chores to pay for his room and board.

At the age of 21, McGuffey left Greersburg and enrolled in Washington College, later known as Washington and Jefferson College. To make expenses, he taught during the winter terms at a district school and then returned to his studies at the college. He eventually graduated in 1826 with a bachelor's degree. Following graduation, he became an instructor at his alma mater, and remained at that position for several years. He also continued his teaching in nearby district schools.

Life-Changing Opportunity

It was at one of these schools in Paris, Kentucky, that his life would change forever. McGuffey's reputation as a teacher had reached the new president of Miami College, Reverend Robert Bishop. Bishop traveled more than 100 miles to observe William's classroom teaching, and was impressed. He then offered McGuffey a position as assistant professor at Miami College for $600 per year (about $15,000 today). While modest, this salary must have seemed like a fortune to the poverty-stricken young man.

With his brother Alexander, William McGuffey traveled more than 300 miles by horseback to his new school. Here he began his successful collegiate teaching career. Soon, he met and married Harriet Spinning, and the three settled into the small college town of Oxford, Ohio. Within just a few years, McGuffey was ordained as a Presbyterian minister and began a family with Harriet.

McGuffey Meets Lyman Beecher

It wasn't long before McGuffey developed a reputation as an educational reformer and advocate for the common school. He had speaking engagements in and around Oxford, and he often gave lectures in Cincinnati. It was here in 1832 that he met Lyman Beecher and his distinguished family.

Lyman Beecher recently had moved from New England to Cincinnati to become the president of Lane Theological Seminary. Beecher, a noted theologian, had developed a reputation as a strong advocate of both temperance and abolition. When his church in Boston burned to the ground because someone had stored whiskey in the basement of the sanctuary, he was outraged and sought another position. He then moved his family to Cincinnati.

The Beecher household consisted of eleven children including seven sons and four daughters. The entourage that accompanied Lyman to the Queen City included his wife Harriet, daughters Catherine and Harriet, as well as several of his young sons.

The Cincinnati Circle

Soon, the Beechers developed an intellectual group of reformers that we call the Cincinnati Circle. It included his two oldest daughters as well as Edward Mansfield, author, editor, and the first superintendent of Ohio's common schools. Other members of this distinguished circle were Albert Picket, an educational writer, and Joseph Ray, author of *Ray's Arithmetic*. Picket and Ray would become close collaborators with McGuffey in developing a curriculum for the nation.

William McGuffey personally was invited by Lyman Beecher to meet with members of the Cincinnati Circle and soon he became a permanent fixture in the group. William developed a deep friendship with many of these educational reformers, including Catherine Beecher.

CATHERINE BEECHER—REFORMER

Catherine Beecher was an important figure in the reform movements of mid-nineteenth century. She fought for temperance and abolition and led protests opposing the policies of "Indian removal" in the early 1830s. As an educational reformer, she was a major figure in the kindergarten movement and a strong supporter of Frederick William Froebel. Like Froebel and Pestalozzi before him, she advocated for the importance of play in early childhood education.

Throughout her long career she also promoted women's education. In 1823, she established the Hartford Female Seminary, where she taught until 1832 when the family moved to Cincinnati. She also was an educational author and self-published a series of elementary arithmetic books, a work on theology, and another on mental and moral philosophy.

When Catherine arrived in Cincinnati in 1832, she established another female seminary but, due to poor health, was forced to close the school after just two years. Nevertheless, she continued to write and advocate for female education and teacher training as well as for schools on the western and southern frontiers. Later she wrote that her goal in life was to "unite American women in an effort to provide a Christian education for two million children in our country."

Truman & Smith Publishers

During these years Catherine had developed a professional relationship with the Truman & Smith publishing house in Cincinnati. The press had expressed to her an interest in publishing a series of educational *Readers* for the common schools in the state, and Catherine recommended that William McGuffey write these books. He gladly accepted the assignment and received $1,000 (the equivalent of $25,000 today) to write and edit four *Readers*, a *Primer* for younger children, and a *Speller*.

Fresh from his success with his *Readers*, McGuffey left Miami College in Oxford and took a position as president of Cincinnati College, where he strengthened his connections and collaboration with members of the Cincinnati Circle, including Ray, Picket, and Mansfield. The McGuffeys actually named their fifth child Edward Mansfield McGuffey in honor of his close friend.

Following the closing of the Cincinnati College, however, McGuffey assumed the position of president of Ohio University in Athens, Ohio. While his work there was extraordinary, he was disliked by some members of the local community because of his policy of prohibiting grazing animals on campus. He left after just a few years and, the story goes, he was heard yelling to his family as they rode out of town: "Don't look back, I don't ever wish to set eyes on that place again." And he never did!

Soon McGuffey and his family traveled to the prestigious University of Virginia in Charlottesville, and he took a position as professor of moral philosophy. McGuffey was the first clergyman to become a professor at the school and helped to mitigate the image of UVA as an "infidel institution." He taught there well into his 70s until he passed in 1873.

JOSEPH RAY

Joseph Ray, another distinguished member of the Cincinnati Circle and close collaborator with William McGuffey, also would publish with Truman & Smith. Joseph had studied medicine and received his degree from the Ohio Medical College at the age of 22. After a short career as a physician, however, he discovered that his real love was math.

As a result, he accepted a position as mathematics teacher at Woodward High School in Cincinnati. In addition to his teaching, Ray's primary focus was the publication of math textbooks that were accessible to the common school students of this period.

Like McGuffey, Ray would help to revolutionize American education. He understood that prior to the turn of the nineteenth century, math was either taught in a theoretical and abstract form or not at all. But as the market revolution spread throughout the country in the first half of the nineteenth century, mathematics had become more important and gradually had made its way into the curriculum of the nation.

Collaboration

During their many discussions in the Cincinnati circle, McGuffey and Ray centered their attention on the importance and practical application of knowledge. In his *Practical Arithmetic*, first published in 1834, Ray focused on the new mathematical elements of the market economy including the buying and selling of commodities such as sugar, tea, coffee, bacon, butter, and beer.

ALBERT PICKET

Albert Picket was yet another important collaborator with McGuffey and Ray. Like the Beechers, Picket had migrated west to Cincinnati and soon became a regular in the emerging Cincinnati Circle. Picket established a school for girls in the Queen City upon his arrival.

Early Educational Reform

Before coming to Cincinnati, Picket was active member of the New York Society of Associated Teachers. He also established the Manhattan School for Girls in 1804. The school closed briefly because of some financial problems but reopened in 1820 with a boys' division. Eventually the institution was successful and enrolled nearly 500 students annually.

Educational Author

Picket also had success with his *Union Spelling Book*, published (ca) 1804. Then, in the next decade, with the help of his son John, he published a series of texts in spelling, reading, and grammar with the general title of *The American School Class-Books*. These books were relatively successful and competed well with Webster's *The Blue Back Speller*.

By 1818, Albert and John Picket were considered two of the foremost educators in New York. That year the two published the first professional journal for teachers in the United States, entitled *The Academician*. The journal centered on the educational theories of Bacon and Locke and routinely published reviews of Pestalozzi and Lancaster, both of whom were still alive at that time. In addition, the *Journal* provided practical advice to teachers.

While the *Journal* suspended publication after just two years, its legacy remained. It was at this point in his career that Picket traveled to Cincinnati where he established his girls school and was introduced to members of the Cincinnati Circle, including his future collaborators Joseph Ray and William McGuffey.

College of Teachers

Together these three reformers worked to establish the College of Teachers, one of the first teacher associations in the nation. Later it would become the Western Literary Institute and the College of Professional Teachers, the forerunner of the National Educational Association.

In 1834, at the age of 63, the aging Picket, with the support of his close collaborators and associates from the Cincinnati Circle (including Lyman Beecher), secured a charter from the Ohio Legislature for a teacher's institute—a normal school. Unfortunately, the school never opened due to financial problems associated with the economic collapse of 1837. Nevertheless, by the time of Picket's death in 1850, at the age of 80, several normal schools had been established in Ohio, while a number of educational journals carried on his pioneering work.

A NEW CURRICULUM

The books of these three educational pioneers—William McGuffey, Joseph Ray, and Albert Picket—would have a dramatic effect on education and would change the way that teachers taught and students learned. The common school now had the basic material for the emerging curriculum of the nation.

MCGUFFEY'S READERS

Like Ray and Picket, McGuffey sought to create texts that were understandable and appropriate for the developing economy and nation. He began to write and edit his books in 1834, and, by 1836, he had published his first two *Readers*. This material was met with immediate critical acclaim, and the books were adopted by common schools throughout the nation.

While the work of both Ray and Picket were important in the shift toward a unified curriculum for the nation, McGuffey and his set of *Readers* stood alone. These *Readers* literally changed how teachers taught and how children learned in a number of important ways.

From Memorization to Comprehension

Perhaps the most important pedagogical contribution of the *Readers* was the shift from memorization to comprehension. McGuffey's "Suggestions for Teachers" encouraged instructors to abandon memorization as the primary form of instruction. He wrote that "nothing can be more fatiguing to the teacher than a recitation." Instead, he urged teachers to "try the conversational method of communicating instruction and training for the mind."

The Child-Centered Approach

Moreover, he wrote that if teachers used the discussion questions at the end of each selection, they could engage their students and move beyond the abstractions of memorization. By using these methods, McGuffey argued that the role of teachers would gradually move from that of a disciplinarian to a facilitator of learning. Moreover, by emphasizing discussion and comprehension rather than memorization, students would be more involved in the learning process.

The Written Exam

In the past, achievement was measured by the ability of a student to memorize spelling words and short passages from their *Readers*. Spelling bee champions often became local heroes and received acclaim from their communities. As teachers understood, however, students who had a knack for memorization were not always the most intelligent in the class.

As Warren Burton, the great mid-nineteenth-century educator, wrote, "Memorus Wordwell" was the reigning spelling champion in his community. But "he did not know at all what the sounds he uttered meant." Clearly, the talent to parrot letters and spell words correctly or the ability to memorize a short scripture from the Bible or a poem did not mean that the reciter understood the material.

Written exams slowly made their way into the classrooms of America. These exams would measure comprehension and understanding, and not simply the ability to memorize. While formal memorization and presentation of speeches with gestures and dramatic effect would continue in the classroom (and were emphasized in McGuffey's fifth *Reader*), reading comprehension measured by written exams (not standardized exams) would become the norm by the late nineteenth and early twentieth centuries.

The Graded Approach to Learning

Another important contribution that McGuffey made with his *Readers* was the graded approach to learning. Each *Reader*, beginning with *The Primer*, was arranged according to the difficulty in understanding the reading material and vocabulary presented. McGuffey recognized, through his own teaching experiences, that while some students were able to memorize passages from classical literature and the Bible, they often had little understanding of the material presented.

The graded *Reader* was a major step in the development of pedagogy in this country. By moving from memorization to understanding, McGuffey helped improve the educational experience of generations of American children.

The Shift to Secular Instruction

William McGuffey was a very religious man. He was an ordained minister of the Presbyterian Church, and he had a strong sense of moral values derived from the Bible. Nevertheless, like others before him, he also understood that students needed to develop a sense of national identity, individual responsibility, and civic virtue.

In traditional society, the Roman Catholic Church (the only Christian church in western Europe prior to the Reformation of the 1500s) had promoted deference to the nobility. The idea of submission to the judgements, values, and ideas of the noble class was generally understood by most members of society.

In the new republic however, Americans had been "cut loose" from our traditional social moorings of deference. Americans, especially children, often had little respect for authority or the moral directions of adults. Many European observers noted that American children frequently were rebellious and sometimes disrespectful, a product associated with their interpretation of democracy and the idea of the absolute equality of all men.

This was a dilemma for teachers in the common schools in the nineteenth century. Earlier, Webster had understood this problem and argued that American students should be instructed in basic subjects, but also have a keen understanding of his or her "moral and social duties." McGuffey would extend these themes in his *Readers*.

Rational Obedience

Rather than memorizing Biblical imperatives to mold their behavior and values, however, McGuffey emphasized the development of what can be seen as "rational obedience" among students. For example, in the first *Reader*, obedience and respect for parents was demonstrated in a number of selections.

In "The Walk," a father demonstrates the marvels of nature to his young son. Then in "The Good Girl," a young girl is taught to sew by her mother. In these stories and others, students were encouraged to respect and obey their parents, not because they were told to or commanded to, but because they understood the importance of parents in their lives.

Once they comprehended the central importance of their parents, students were in a better position to obey secular authorities such as the police, government officials, their employers and, of course, their teachers! In later *Readers*, students would read selections that would help extend this understanding to a love of country and respect for their political leaders. In short, while religion was not eliminated from the McGuffey *Readers*, social and moral values were taught in a more secular context.

Individual Responsibility

McGuffey clearly understood that if students did not have the Bible to guide their actions and shape their moral behavior, they must develop in themselves a strong sense of individual responsibility. This would be based on temperance, kindness, inclusion, and most importantly, the limits of their own self-interest.

Temperance

For McGuffey, individual responsibility began with temperance. Although often seen as a religious value, temperance was in fact a secular one proposed in part by the emerging market economy and promoted by reformers during this period. Temperate workers were reliable and steady workers. They were good to their families, and they often had a solid moral compass.

In his first *Reader*, McGuffey included a story entitled "Don't Take Strong Drink." Then in "The Whiskey Boy," students were warned of the dangers of drinking alcohol. Here little John "got tipsy every day." By the age of eight he had become a drunkard. Eventually little John was found drunk in the street, brought to a poor house, and died within two weeks. Students were then asked rhetorically, "How do you think his father felt now?"

Kindness

In addition to temperance, McGuffey promoted the idea of kindness. In many of his selections, kindness was the central theme. In the first *Reader*, for example, 17 of the 45 selections focused on kindness. Student were encouraged to be kind to all living things including cows, oxen, cats, dogs, birds, and even insects.

The Limits of Self-Interest

By developing the idea that kindness was important, students would begin to see the limits of their own self-interest. Clearly, there was more to life than what you wanted to do! In "The Cruel Boy," for example, George Craft liked to pull the wings off flies. One day, another boy explained to him that it was cruel to act that way. George apparently learned his lesson and stopped torturing insects.

Kindness to People

Once this basic idea of kindness was illustrated, McGuffey expanded this idea by including lessons on kindness to people. Two selections from the first two *Readers* illustrate how McGuffey promoted these ideas. The first was "Never Do Mischief." A group of young boys out to have some fun dressed up in white sheets and frightened Henry, one of their classmates. Henry was traumatized and became what McGuffey referred to as an "idiot." Recognizing the consequences of their actions, the boys were ashamed and changed their behavior.

In the second *Reader*, McGuffey included a selection entitled "The Boys Who Did Mischief for Fun." In this story, two boys stretched a "grass rope" across a path and waited to see people "tumble on their noses." First came a farmer who fell flat on his face, then a milkmaid who stumbled and spilled her milk.

Finally, a man came running down the path, tripped on the rope, sprained his ankle, and was unable to walk. As the boys laughed in glee, they discovered that the man was on his way to fetch a doctor to save the life of the father of one of the boys. Laughter now turned to horror!

Inclusion

And then there was a story in the fifth *Reader* that integrated the ideas of both kindness and acceptance of immigrants to this country, entitled "The Pathetic Migrant." A family of migrants was traveling from Maine to Illinois. These were poor people and many along the way laughed at them and joked about their clothes and their accents.

To make matters worse, their horse broke through a rotten bridge and drowned. Despite the rounds of laughter from some onlookers, one man gave the father 10 dollars so the family could continue their long journey. The group eventually reached Illinois and their leader became a "thriving farmer and a neighbor to him who was a friend in need and a friend indeed." This story certainly had an impact on many of the students who read it.

Nationalism and Love of Country

Finally, McGuffey included a number of stories that promoted both nationalism and love of country. He integrated numerous passages about the Founding Fathers including George Washington, Paul Revere, Alexander Hamilton, Thomas Jefferson, and Benjamin Franklin. Some of these stories and poems were historically accurate; others, apocryphal. Paul Revere's "midnight ride" was celebrated, as was George Washington's famous cherry tree incident: "I cannot lie father, I cut the tree."

One poem titled "What I Live For" would inspire generations of American students to support and honor the brave men and women who made our nation great.

> I live to learn their story
> Who suffered for my sake
> To emulate their glory
> And Follow in their wake
> The noble of all ages
> Whose deed crown history's pages
> And times great volume make.

MCGUFFEY'S LEGACY

These and other stories in the McGuffey *Readers* augmented academic learning and helped to mold young boys and girls into patriotic citizens. By beginning with the ideas of kindness and the importance of family and parents, then moving on to the value of individual responsibility and finally to love of country, McGuffey helped to create a curriculum for the new nation.

Limitations of the *Readers*

And yet, while the importance of the McGuffey *Readers* cannot be overstated, "Old Guff" was a product of his times. Clearly, this was a white man's world. No African Americans, free or enslaved, made their way into the *Readers*. Moreover, while young girls and their mothers were mentioned in a number of stories, the *Readers* generally focused on men and boys.

And while many of the values introduced by McGuffey were good ones, beliefs such as temperance that were promoted by Protestant sects tended to alienate new immigrant groups, including the Irish and Germans. Moreover, the Vulgate Bible (Roman Catholic Bible) was never mentioned, and the *Readers* presented a vision of the nation that was white, pan-Protestant, and "native."

A CURRICULUM FOR THE NATION: A COLLABORATION

The collaboration of William McGuffey, Joseph Ray, and Albert Picket was a sensation. Together they created a curriculum for the nation. Slowly, beginning in the 1830s through the rest of the nineteenth century, American common school students were introduced to the value-driven stories, poems, and speeches that McGuffey selected. They learned basic mathematics from Ray's *Practical Arithmetic*, which validated the new emerging market economy. Finally, through Picket's *The American School Class-Books*, students were introduced to reading, spelling, and grammar. The nation now had a unified curriculum to support its common schools.

Chapter 7

Freedmen's Bureau Schools

By the mid-nineteenth century, the United States had made considerable yet limited progress in public education. Collaboration among intellectuals, educational reformers, philosophers, politicians, and grassroots organizers had slowly begun to transform education in this country.

INTELLECTUAL COLLABORATION

In the late eighteenth century, the collaboration of intellectuals such as John Locke, Jean-Jacques Rousseau, Johann Pestalozzi, and Voltaire provided a new perspective on education. This included the methods of teaching, the treatment and discipline of children, the importance of a child-centered approach to education, and the separation of church and schools.

ADVOCATES OF THE POOR

Educational reformers at the turn of the nineteenth century such as Joseph Lancaster collaborated with his Quaker colleagues to provide an education for the children of a new class of industrial workers in both England and the United States. Their work alerted the American people of the need to teach the poor. Along the way, some of Lancaster's innovative methods of teaching slowly made their way into the classrooms of America.

GENDER EQUITY

By the early 1820s, reformers such as Emma Willard fought for equal access to education for women. Willard collaborated with family members and students to establish the Troy Female Seminary in 1821; her work helped

Figure 7.1. Freedmen's Bureau school, James Plantation, North Carolina. Photo, 1866. https://commons.wikimedia.org/wiki/File:Freedmen%27s_School,_James_Plantation,_North_Carolina.png.

Americans recognize the abilities of women as compared to men. She also swung open the door to female teacher education, anticipating the normal school movement decades later.

THE COMMON SCHOOL

Then, in the 1830s, the collaboration of politicians, commercial farmers, small business owners, workingmen organizations, and educational reformers like Horace Mann worked to establish the common school. When Mann was appointed as secretary of the Massachusetts Board of Education in 1837, he brought a new perspective on education to America. He demonstrated that schools were not only places of learning but also centers of inclusion, equity, and patriotism. Mann also helped promote the idea of the public's responsibility to support schools financially and provide for teacher training.

A CURRICULUM FOR THE NATION

As the common school began to take shape throughout the nation, there also was a growing need for a unified curriculum that would help children learn and develop the values of inclusion, rational obedience, individual responsibility, kindness, the limits of self-interest, as well as love of country.
　The collaboration of Joseph Ray, who provided common school students with a graded, market-oriented approach to math; Albert Picket, who fashioned a secularized speller for young children; and William McGuffey, who wrote and edited a series of *Readers* that promoted the values of the new republic, the common school now had the basic components of a unified curriculum for American children.

ORIGINAL SIN OF EDUCATION

But the "original sin" of American education was the exclusion of enslaved and free blacks from schools throughout the nation. In the colonial South, for example, black children had virtually no educational opportunities except for the occasional goodwill of a slave owner or a handful of charity schools for free blacks.
　By the beginning of the nineteenth century, however, things became even more dire. Two slave uprisings in the 1820s and 1830s led southern legislators to pass laws designed to punish black people who dared learn to read. In North Carolina, as just one example, the penalty for a white person who taught enslaved blacks to read was a fine of $100–$200 or imprisonment. Free blacks who were caught teaching slaves could receive 20–39 lashes, and a slave violating the law would get "39 lashes on his or her bare back."
　In the North, some educational opportunities existed for free black children, but were extremely limited. A few communities allowed integrated schools, but most were segregated throughout the nineteenth century. In New York, for example, a law was passed in 1823 that established a handful of schools exclusively for the "colored race." This law remained in effect for many years.
　There was some support for African American education among progressives and religious groups. As we have seen, the Quakers and the New York Manumission Society continued their support for black education (enslaved or free) throughout this period. They also established the famous African Free School in the late eighteenth century that merged with New York Public Schools in 1835.

AFRICAN AMERICAN ADVOCACY FOR EDUCATION

But the primary support for African American education came from within the black community. Black preachers often doubled as teachers and held classes following their Sunday sermons. Through their efforts, along with support from the black community and a handful of white supporters, they were able to establish schools throughout the North and border states prior to the Civil War.

ANTEBELLUM BLACK EDUCATION

The African Methodist Episcopal (AME) Church as well as progressive northern Baptists also established hundreds of small black schools throughout this period. In Baltimore, Maryland, for example, Protestant organizations founded the Sharp Street Methodist Episcopal Church's Free African School in 1802.

Ten years later, Daniel Coker founded the Bethel Charity School for free African Americans, and, in 1824, the St. James Protestant Episcopal Day School was founded for free blacks in the region. Several other schools for African American children would be established during this period.

Then, in 1828, Mother Mary Lange and a group of Roman Catholic nuns from Baltimore established the St. Francis Academy for the secondary education of "colored girls." The school's primary mission was to "teach children of color to read the Bible." The academy was remarkable in a number of ways. Not only did it provide a secondary education for black children, but it challenged the laws of Maryland by teaching enslaved blacks. The St. Francis Academy graduated its first class in 1832 and has continued its educational mission to the present day.

Mother Mary Lange remained with the school until her death in 1882, and today the Roman Catholic Church is honoring her lifelong work in education with the cause for beatification—that is, a step toward sainthood. Mother Mary Lange would be the first female black Saint in the Roman Catholic Church.

WHITE BACKLASH TO BLACK EDUCATION

But even with these modest achievements, the path to African American education was slow and dangerous. The work of Prudence Campbell, a Quaker, illustrates some of these difficulties. Prudence had established a school for girls in Canterbury, Connecticut, in 1831. The Canterbury Female Boarding School had some success and enrolled more than 40 students.

When she admitted Sarah Harris, a 20-year-old African American woman, however, white parents began to withdraw their children from the school. Prudence did not back down, but she reorganized the school as "Miss Crandall's School for Young Ladies and Little Misses of Color." This school had short-lived success and enrolled more than 20 African American girls

Its very success, however, fueled a racist backlash from prominent members of the community. For example, her neighbor, Andrew Judson, led a movement to remove the school from Canterbury, and as a state legislator he helped pass the Connecticut "Black Law" of 1833. This law prohibited schools from teaching African American students from outside the state without town permission.

Once again, Prudence did not comply, was arrested, and spent a night in the county jail. She refused bail but rather sought public support. However, trouble did not stop there. Soon the entire community mobilized against her. Shops were closed to her and her students, doctors refused to treat her sick students and, unbelievably, townspeople poisoned the school's well with animal feces! But when vandals broke all the windows and set fire to the school in the dead of night, she was forced to leave town with a handful of her students.

A TURNING POINT: THE CIVIL WAR

But the turning point for African American education emerged from the ashes of the American Civil War. When Union forces captured most of the ports of the Confederacy by 1862, a groundswell of interest in providing education for African Americans swept through abolitionist organizations in the North. The public/private collaboration between religious groups and secular abolitionists was remarkable.

EARLY CHURCH ADVOCACY

In 1862, for example, New England's Freedmen's Association and the Boston Education Commission sent several hundred white teachers to Hilton Head, South Carolina, which had been recently liberated by the North. The success of this effort led to a number of similar outreach programs. Groups such as the Philadelphia Freedmen's Relief Association, for example, was chartered by the Port Royal Relief Committee. And by the end of the war, this organization had established schools for freedmen (recently freed blacks) throughout the former Confederacy.

As expected, Quakers also were active with their educational efforts. The Friends Association for the Aid and Elevation of the Freedmen, for example, founded 14 schools in Virginia and South Carolina ports during this period. Paralleling these efforts, the African Civilization Society taught more than 8,000 black children and employed more than 125 teachers by the end of the war.

FREEDMEN'S BUREAU SCHOOLS

While these diverse groups were essential in kickstarting the development of African American education during the Civil War itself, the Freedmen's Bureau schools were a powerful collaborative force once the war ended.

The Freedmen's Bureau was a U.S. government agency initiated by President Lincoln and formally established by Congress on March 3, 1865. It had a number of important roles. The first was to "direct provisions, clothing and fuel . . . for the immediate and temporary shelter of destitute and suffering refugees and freedmen and their wives and children." It also became a formal court to settle land disputes between white planters and the freedmen.

Its most important function, however, from our perspective, was the establishment of the Freedmen's Bureau schools. As we have seen, no southern state in the former Confederacy had a system of universal, state-supported public education despite the dramatic growth of common schools in the north. While the movement toward the education of freedmen in some liberated southern coastal communities during the war had promise, there was a great deal left to do.

OLIVER OTIS HOWARD

In 1865, shortly after the war ended, Oliver Otis Howard was appointed as the commissioner of the Freedmen's Bureau. He set up four divisions: Government Control of Lands, Records, Financial Affairs, and Medical Affairs. The Freedmen's Bureau schools became part of the Records Division.

To support these schools, the bureau confiscated property that included planter's mansions, government buildings, books, and furniture. In addition, Howard used the resources of the Freedmen's Bureau to provide funds for transportation as well as room and board for teachers.

Howard also was instrumental in the public/private collaboration of the federal government with religious organizations that had spearheaded freedmen's education during the war. His work with the American Missionary Association and the First Congregational Society of Washington, for example, helped to establish 11 black colleges to prepare teachers for schools throughout the South. These included Fisk, Atlanta, and Tugaloo. And when a freedmen's college was founded in Washington, DC, on March 2, 1867, it was formally named Howard University.

BUREAU SUPPORT OF BLACK EDUCATION

Overall, the Freedmen's Bureau spent $5 million (the equivalent of $90 million today) to establish schools in the South. In some communities, the Freedmen's Bureau schools published their own textbooks. These books emphasized a "bootstrap philosophy" that encouraged black children to work hard and achieve, both in school and in life.

Freedmen's Bureau *Readers* typically had traditional lessons that focused on patriotism with special emphasis on Abraham Lincoln, the Great Emancipator. They also included excerpts from the Bible and biographies of famous African Americans such as abolitionist Frederick Douglass. Finally, these *Readers* emphasized values such as humility, a strong work ethic, and temperance.

"A VERITABLE FEVER" FOR EDUCATION

By the end of 1865, the Freedmen's Bureau had enrolled more than 90,000 formerly enslaved black and impoverished white children in these schools. As Booker T. Washington noted later, these schools created "a veritable fever" for education among former slaves.

At the peak of the Freedmen's Bureau school direct efforts, about 9,000 teachers had been recruited to teach in these schools. Once again, the public/private collaboration of the Freedmen's Bureau with various religious and secular organizations in both the North and South helped to recruit teachers to participate in this grand and idealistic social experiment.

DEMOGRAPHY OF BUREAU TEACHERS

Overall, about half of the Freedmen's Bureau teachers were southern whites, about a third were black, mostly from the South, and about 15 percent were northern whites. In addition, there were some abolitionists among this group, most of whom hailed from New England.

Southern men outnumbered women teachers, and it appears that in addition to humanitarianism, their motivation to teach was also the relatively high salaries offered them by the Freedmen's Bureau. On the other hand, those who came from the north were often quite idealistic and were sponsored and paid by churches and abolitionist organizations.

MARY BOWSER: AFRICAN AMERICAN TEACHER

Among the 9,000 teachers that taught in the Freedmen's Bureau schools was Mary Bowser. Bowser was born a slave in Richmond, Virginia. Her owner, Mrs. Van Lew, was a progressive woman and recognized that Mary was a precocious child. She sent the girl to Philadelphia for an education and, at the age of 14, Bowser went to Liberia with a group of missionaries to do outreach work.

Bowser returned to Virginia on the eve of the American Civil War and for the next several years she reportedly spied for the Union Army. She also did some clandestine teaching until the end of the conflict. Then when the Freedmen's Bureau schools were established in 1865, she joined with others to teach emancipated children and adults.

In 1867, Bowser left Virginia and founded a Freedmen's Bureau school in St. Marys, Georgia. There she taught 70 day students, a dozen adult night students, and 100 Sunday school students. All this was done on a shoestring budget with few books and virtually no teaching supplies. Moreover, she had to contend with a bitter white community.

Fear of White Racism

Bowser expressed her fears in a letter to Superintendent Everhardt of the Georgia Freedmen's Bureau. She wrote, "I wish there was some law here or some protection (from local whites who) exhibit a sinister expression about the eye and the quiet but bitterly expressed feeling that I know portends evil . . . with a little whiskey in them they dare do anything."

Later that year, Bowser married Mr. Garvin, and wrote to Superintendent Everhardt with the good news. She asked him to address her in the future by her married name. Mary Garvin continued to teach for the next several months while her husband was in Cuba and, later, was directed by the Bureau to close the school because Georgia had established its own "system of education." The Bureau would officially end its idealistic educational experiment throughout the former Confederacy in 1870.

THE "MISSES COOKES"

Two white women from Richmond, Virginia, known as "The Misses Cookes," also taught in the Freedmen's Bureau schools. During the war the sisters had established a school in their home and, when the war ended, the Freedmen's Bureau recruited them to teach in the newly created Chimborazo School in the city. The school was part of the former Chimborazo Hospital, the largest facility of its kind in the Confederacy.

The sisters gladly accepted the invitation, and by November 1865, they had enrolled more than 300 students ranging in age from 4 to 29. The school operated for the next five years until it was absorbed by the city of Richmond's newly established school system. All told, the sisters were responsible for the education of hundreds of black children and young adults in this important Freedmen's Bureau school.

CATHERINE BENT

While Mary Bowser and the Cooke sisters hailed from the South, Miss Catherine Bent was from Newburyport, Massachusetts, and went south to teach. While others were recruited directly by the Freedmen's Bureau itself, Catherine was sent by the National Freedmen's Relief Association of New York. This group was organized by the American Missionary Association and the Congregationalist Church. Together they sent hundreds of teachers south to augment the work of the Freedmen's Bureau.

Catherine was assigned to a "school" in Gainesville, Florida, where she taught "sixty negro pupils" in a "unfinished dilapidated church building with no doors or windows." Like other teachers during this period, Catherine also experienced the bitter resentment of the local white community.

A "Ladylike Person"

Mr. Cyrus Woodman, a northern land speculator who passed through Gainesville during this period, wrote in 1867 that "Miss Bent was in her second year of teaching and was residing with a German family. She lives more or less in isolation. The white ladies of Gainesville refuse to speak to her, and (as a result) she has stopped going to church." Woodman praised her teaching under these conditions and noted, "She keeps an excellent school and is a modest, unassuming, ladylike person."

Catherine and Harriet

Miss Catherine Bent was indeed an excellent teacher, and enrolled so many children that the Freedmen's Bureau sent Miss Harriet Barnes of Norwalk, Connecticut, to assist her. Together the two enrolled hundreds of students who eagerly learned to read and cipher.

Despite their success, Catherine and Harriet were often taunted by white boys who harassed them and threw rocks at the school. In fact, the teachers were nearly hit by rocks on a regular basis. The white boys were encouraged by the community when they heard black students singing songs such as "Rally Round the Flag Boys." Moreover, they felt that the teachers were spreading Republican Party propaganda that would undermine their political power.

Nevertheless, Catherine and Harriet pushed on and were quite successful. Freedmen's bureau superintendent of Florida, Mr. Durkee, wrote to his superior that their closing exercises in June 1867 were attended by several prominent white men in the community. He also noted that the students were orderly and well-disciplined, and he felt that they had a strong desire to learn.

The Union Academy

By October 1867, a group of middle-class Gainesville blacks formed a Board of Trustees with the intension of building a new, permanent school building. It would be known as the Union Academy. They purchased land, drew up architectural plans for the building, and, with the financial support of the Freedmen's Bureau, were able to purchase "doors, sashes, windows, desks and a stove from Jacksonville."

Local black artisans volunteered their labor and built a beautiful structure measuring 70 by 30 feet with a piazza, a belfry, and a bell that could be "heard for at least two miles." The interior of the school had two blackboards and a sliding partition that allowed for graded instruction. Later the trustees purchased a "parlor organ" for student lessons and entertainment.

The Union Academy was by all accounts a success as both a high school and a normal school. Catherine Bent and Harriet Barnes personally trained a handful of bright students to become teachers. Bent reported to her superiors that "51 of her 100 pupils were able to read very well with 38 of them reading at an advanced level, 31 studied arithmetic and 14 were learning geography."

Small Successes

In her humble way, Bent wrote that "I am well satisfied with the progress that the children are making . . . and whatever knowledge they acquire is by hard labor." Beyond their academic work, she also noted that students were learning the values of sobriety, thrift, industry, and order.

During the 1868–1869 school year, both Bent and Barnes left the Union Academy for other positions. Bent traveled south to Ocala, Florida, to teach and Barnes returned to her home in Norwalk, Connecticut. Replacing them was difficult, but two other white teachers were recruited by the American Missionary Association. Maggie Gardner and Emma B. Eveleth carried on their work teaching 179 pupils, with the assistance of two black teachers, Eliza James and Lawrence Chestnut.

SARAH JANE FOSTER: YANKEE SCHOOLMARM

Sarah Jane Foster was yet another idealistic Freedmen's Bureau teacher. She was born in Gray, Maine, on October 12, 1839, into a large, hardworking middle class family.

As a young woman, Foster wrote short stories and taught for a time in a common school in Maine. She belonged to the local Free Will Baptist Church, a bastion of abolitionism during this period. Her exposure to these ideas clearly had a dramatic impression on the young girl and, when the opportunity arose, she was determined to go south to teach.

"Mission Teacher to the Freedmen"

In early November 1865, Foster left home and journeyed to Martinsburg, West Virginia, as a "Mission teacher to the Freedmen." She sailed on the *Chesapeake* and the captain gave her and four other mission teachers (assigned to schools in Savannah and Wilmington) free passage to Harpers Ferry, Virginia. There Foster met Reverend N. C. Brackett, who was coordinating the mission schools.

From Harpers Ferry, she and another teacher, Anna Wright, traveled by stagecoach to Martinsburg, about 20 miles away. They were accompanied on this leg of their journey by Lieutenant Smith and Mr. Brackett. Both women were determined to get started and "begin their labors today."

Grueling Teaching Schedule

Martinsburg had only one schoolhouse in the town, but the two women were determined to enroll as many students as possible and eventually open another school as well. They taught four-hour sessions each day for children, and three times a week they taught evening sessions for adult learners. Foster taught in the "uncommonly bad" basement classroom of the school that "lacked a blackboard and sufficient textbooks." Each day she taught 80 students, and 45 more in each night session.

Constant Humiliation

Despite her idealistic enthusiasm, Foster endured constant humiliation and could not find accommodations in her community. In 1866, she noted in her diary that she had been "slandered by the mob" and accused of sexual impropriety because she had been walking "arm and arm with colored men." These "men," however, were in fact her black students escorting her as she walked back and forth to school.

As a result of these baseless accusations, however, Foster was forced out of her boarding house and eventually moved in with "Mrs. Bayles," who was "not afraid much of public scorn, having once taught the blacks here herself."

Fired by the Bureau!

Soon thereafter, Foster was transferred to Harpers Ferry, where she taught for several months. Then on her summer leave, she returned to Maine to visit her family where she received a letter of dismissal from the Bureau. Apparently, the baseless accusations of sexual misconduct had had its pernicious effect.

She Gave Her Life to Teaching

Undeterred, Foster appealed to the American Missionary Society and was hired as a teacher in Charleston Neck, South Carolina. There she taught on an isolated farm, far from the viciousness of local disgruntled former Confederates. But trouble found its way to Foster, and after just a month she contracted yellow fever, returned to her home in Maine, and died shortly thereafter on June 25, 1868. It's no exaggeration to say that Sarah Jane Foster gave her life to teaching.

GROWING OPPOSITION TO THE FREEDMEN'S BUREAU SCHOOLS

Despite the enthusiasm and great success of the Freedmen's Bureau schools, there was a continuing chorus of opposition to them from the southern white community. Residents of southern communities were often appalled when they discovered that "Yankee schoolmarms" were teaching black children that they were "equal" to whites and that the Republican Party (the party of Lincoln) was their friend.

And even the most tolerant southern whites were angered when they passed a schoolhouse and heard black children singing "John Brown's Body" or "Marching through Georgia." As a result, some Freedmen's Bureau schools were burned, a handful of male teachers were tarred and feathered, while others were beaten by mobs. Men and women teachers like Sarah Jane Foster often were denied accommodations in local boarding houses and hotels, and they were harassed and intimidated by members of the community as they walked in public.

THE ROLE OF "REDEEMERS"

By the early 1870s, southern Democrats, often referred to as "Redeemers," grew in strength and numbers. As southern states abided by the Reconstruction requirements to be readmitted into the union, these Democratic "Redeemers" slowly regained control of their state legislatures from Republicans and began sending Democratic representatives to Congress.

WHITE SUPREMACY

At the same time, groups such as the Ku Klux Klan, the Red Shirts of Mississippi and North Carolina, and the White League of Louisiana grew in strength and numbers, promoting white supremacy and spreading violence in black communities. Moreover, as a visible sign of Republican Party control, the vulnerable schoolteacher was often the target of harassment and intimidation by these groups.

By 1876, all but three states of the former Confederacy had been "redeemed," and the contested election that year resulted in a compromise that essentially ended Reconstruction. Most northerners had become weary of the battle over Reconstruction as well. An entire generation had endured constant political vitriol and bitter divisions within the country. Then the war itself had eviscerated the nation as democracy trembled in the breach. Many northerners said "enough is enough."

"A BRIEF MOMENT IN THE SUN"

As a result, Democratic control of the South returned and there was vengeance in the air. As W. E. B. DuBois noted later, "The slave went free, stood a brief moment in the sun; then moved back again toward slavery." And so it seemed for African American education as well.

And yet, despite the racism, violence, hate, and indifference, African American education somehow persisted and grew slowly. The efforts of black people themselves, aided by progressive black and white churches as well as philanthropic organizations, now took center stage as the federal government essentially turned its back on the freedmen.

A BRIGHT SPOT: HBCU

For a time, small, dilapidated primary schoolhouses dotted the rural landscape of the South. They represented evidence of the exciting days of the Freedmen's Bureau. But by the late 1870s, even these were rapidly disappearing. And yet, one bright spot was the growth of black colleges and universities. Today, 107 of these colleges and universities remain active, many of which were founded during Reconstruction and the dark days of Jim Crow.

Among these important institutions are Atlanta University, now Clark Atlanta University, founded in 1865; Howard University in Washington, DC, founded in 1867; Morehouse College (for men) in Atlanta, 1867; Hampton Agricultural and Industrial School, now Hampton University, in Hampton, Virginia, in 1868; Scotia Seminary, now Barber-Scotia College, in Concord, North Carolina, in 1870; and Spelman College (for women) in Atlanta, in 1881.

TUSKEGEE UNIVERSITY

One of the most visible and important black colleges formed during this period, however, was Tuskegee University, founded in 1881. The school was established as part of a collaboration between the Democratic candidate for the Alabama State House, Colonial W. F. Foster, and Lewis Adams, as well as black leaders from Macon County, Alabama.

In 1881, funds were allocated for the Tuskegee Normal School for Colored Teachers. Black leaders contacted Hampton College to recruit a principal for their new school, and soon thereafter a young 25-year-old teacher by the name of Booker T. Washington was hired.

BOOKER T. WASHINGTON

In 1882, the school purchased an abandoned plantation of about 100 acres, and Washington began his tenure at the school. Booker T. Washington had been trained at Hampton Agricultural and Industrial School and was committed to providing black students with occupational skills that would help them get jobs once they left Tuskegee. This vocational approach was the core of the curriculum at the school, though teacher training also became an important function of the school as well.

"Sainted Philanthropists"

While Washington was a gifted teacher and administrator, he excelled as a fundraiser for the school. He and second wife, Olivia America Davidson, spent most of their energies courting what he called his "sainted philanthropists." These included some of the wealthiest industrialists and businessmen of the Gilded Age, such as Andrew Carnegie, Colis Huntington, John Rockefeller, Jacob Schiff, and Julius Rosenwald.

These benefactors were impressed with Washington's self-help philosophy and his administrative skills. The "bootstrap" approach of Tuskegee appealed to donors who were willing to "help those who helped themselves."

JULIUS ROSENWALD

One of Washington's most generous benefactors was Julius Rosenwald. Rosenwald was a "self-made man" who became the leader of Sears and Roebuck stores in Chicago, one of the most successful department store chains in the country. Washington and Rosenwald developed a strong relationship, and Rosenwald agreed to become a member of the Board of Directors of Tuskegee.

In addition to his generous support of the school, Rosenwald also funded the Hampton Institute. Then, in 1912, he began an innovative educational pilot program designed to establish model rural schools. He collaborated with Tuskegee students who not only designed the schools, but also helped to construct them.

Although Washington died suddenly in 1915, Rosenwald continued the efforts of their unique collaboration. He established an endowment fund for the continued growth of black schools throughout the South. He required that local communities match these funds to help establish a collaborative environment between blacks and whites. The program was an enormous success, and by the 1930s, it had led to the creation of more than 5,000 small community schools with supporting resources.

MARY BETHUNE

While Booker T. Washington's collaboration with Julius Rosenwald stands as a model of cooperation for the advancement of black education, there were others. One of the most important of these individuals was Mary Bethune.

Mary received her teacher training at North Carolina's Scotia Seminary in the mid-1890s. Upon graduation she taught for a number of years and then traveled to Daytona, Florida, where she founded the Educational and Industrial Training School for Negro Girls in 1904. Within a year, more than 30 young girls had been admitted to the school. Like Washington before her, she courted wealthy white organizations and invited wealthy white men to sit on the school's Board of Directors.

Among her important benefactors were James Gamble of Procter and Gamble, and Thomas H. White of White Sewing Machines. Her most generous sponsor, however, was John D. Rockefeller, who awarded her school $62,000.

BLACK PHILANTHROPY

In addition to these wealthy white philanthropists were a handful of successful black entrepreneurs who supported African American education during this period. Among these was Madame C. J. Walker. Madame Walker was an orphan and child farm laborer who emerged from poverty to create an enormously successful hair care company for black women in Indianapolis, Indiana. She also trained hundreds of black women to become hair stylists.

But Madame Walker was also a benefactor to black education. She donated to Washington's Tuskegee Institute and Mary McLeod Bethune's Daytona Normal and Industrial Institute. She also contributed to the Palmer Memorial Institute in North Carolina. Her generosity provided yet another model for black philanthropy that would continue.

CONTEMPORARY COLLABORATIVE PHILANTHROPY

The Great Depression of the 1930s, followed by the devastation of World War II, had a detrimental effect on philanthropy in the United States. And despite the dramatic recovery of the nation's economy after the war, the passionate giving from the Rosenwald fund, the Rockefeller foundation, and other institutions began to disappear.

Then, with the *Brown v. Board of Education* decisions of 1954 and 1955, the context of black education changed. It would of course take years before schools throughout America would be desegregated, but the door to equal education of African American children had been opened—if only slightly. The need to support black schools would continue, but there was a feeling that since things were much better, there was less need for philanthropy.

And yet, even after the monumental *Brown* decisions, historically black colleges and universities (HBCUs) continued to struggle financially. Many white philanthropists felt that since the era of segregated schools seemed to have passed, their work was completed, and funding tended to diminish.

UNITED NEGRO COLLEGE FUND

In 1944, the collaboration of three African Americans—William J. Trent, civil rights activist; Frederick D. Patterson, president of the Tuskegee Institute; and Mary McLeod Bethune, founder of Bethune College, brought together the presidents of HBCUs to create the United Negro College Fund. This collaborative effort was designed to "appeal to the national conscience" and to create "strong citadels of learning, carriers of the American dream, (and) seedbeds of social evolution and revolution."

The UNCF, as it was called until 1964, was a huge collaborative effort. It reminded Americans of the needs of HBCUs and that the job was far from complete. In the first 20 years of its existence, the UNCF raised more than $78 million that financed black colleges throughout the nation.

Donations from then Senator John F. Kennedy, who gave his proceeds from his Pulitzer Prize–winning book *Profile in Courage*, as well as an enormous grant of $50 million from Walter Annenberg, had a major impact on fundraising during the 1960s and 1970s. Then, in 1980, fundraising skyrocketed when Lou Rawls began his "Lou Rawl's Parade of Stars," now known as "An Evening of Stars," to alert Americans of the needs of HBCUs. All told, the event has raised more than $200 million.

Since then, fundraisers including the "Walk for Education" in Los Angeles, California, as well as the Cypresswood Golf Tournament in Houston, Texas, have raised both funds and awareness of the needs of black colleges. Funds have been donated from both the conservative Koch Foundation ($25 million) as well as Netflix CEO Reed Hastings and his wife Patty Quillin's generous contributions of $120 million in 2020 for HBCU scholarships.

SUCCESSFUL COLLABORATION

Since the early years of the nineteenth century to the present day, Americans have successfully collaborated to provide education for enslaved and freedmen children, primary and secondary education. For years, churches and abolitionist groups with meager resources but idealistic enthusiasm worked to correct the injustices of slavery and racism.

For a brief moment following the American Civil War, the federal government though the Freedmen's Bureau Schools collaborated with these groups to create what Booker T. Washington called a "veritable fever for education." These schools laid the foundation of both public education in the South as well as the creation of a number of African American colleges that would train teachers for the future.

When Reconstruction ended and the Freedmen's Bureau was abandoned, things looked bleak for African American education. But the collaborative work of black educators such as Booker T. Washington, Mary Bethune, and others encouraged needed philanthropy. The generosity of Julius Rosenwald, John Rockefeller, and others helped to sustain black education during the first decades of Jim Crow era.

Philanthropy declined by the mid-twentieth century, but black educators then established the United Negro College Fund to alert Americans of the needs of black colleges and their students. This collaborative effort has taken off and now provides a significant portion of the funding for these schools.

Clearly, the collaboration among the federal government, religious and secular organizations, African American activists, and generous philanthropists have supported black education throughout the years and has transformed the lives of millions of black Americans. While there clearly is a great deal to do, this collaborative template will provide guidance as we move further into the twenty-first century.

Chapter 8

The Progressives

As Jim Crow raged throughout the nation in the late nineteenth century, and African Americans struggled to provide an education for their children, the common school movement had taken root and was firmly established in many communities throughout the nation. In one-room schoolhouses throughout the countryside and in graded classrooms in American cities, schoolteachers taught mostly white boys and girls the basics, the values of the marketplace, and the importance of patriotism.

Figure 8.1. University of Chicago Laboratory Schools today. Photograph, 2006. https://commons.wikimedia.org/wiki/File:University_of_Chicago_Laboratory_Schools_exterior.jpg.

CHALLENGES OF THE COMMON SCHOOL

But while the common school appeared to meet the needs of mid- to late-nineteenth-century Americans, changes in our economy, society, and demography called for fundamental transformation of our educational system as well.

Economic Change

By the end of the nineteenth century, the American economy had grown dramatically, and it was one of the strongest in the world. It had become more complex and integrated, and the corporation had become the predominant form of economic organization. Schools, however, had not kept pace with these changes and continued to focus on a more rudimentary understanding of marketplace realities.

Demographic Change

Similarly, the demographic composition of the nation also had changed. In the early nineteenth century, the United States was a rural country with only about 5 percent of the population living in cities. By 1900 we were well on our way to becoming an urban nation. In fact, by 1920, about half of the population of the United States lived in our booming cities. Nevertheless, the common school curriculum remained focused on a more pastoral vision of the nation.

Changes in Ethnic and Racial Identity

In addition to the dramatic changes in both our economy and demography was the transformation of our ethnic and racial identity. As African Americans experienced the ravages of racism in rural southern communities, many migrated to urban centers both in the South and in the North. This migration continued well into the twentieth century and peaked during World War I and the 1920s.

In addition to the "great migration" of black Americans was a monumental immigration of millions of Europeans and Asians to this nation. Searching for jobs, religious and political freedom, as well as education for their children, two major waves of immigrants came to these shores.

The first was in mid-nineteenth century when Irish and German people fled their country because of both famine and war. The second and larger wave of southern and eastern European people as well as thousands of Asians arrived in the last decades of the nineteenth century, seeking economic security and educational opportunity. This wave peaked in about 1900 with approximately 1 million immigrants arriving each year.

Once again, because of these fundamental changes the common school and the graded school no longer met the needs of the nation. While the school curriculum centered on the values of pan-Protestantism, the new multicultural realities facing the nation demonstrated that this approach was incomplete and often inappropriate.

Blacks enrolled in northern schools found the cultural values embedded in the McGuffey *Readers* and other textbooks alien to their way of life. Similarly, Roman Catholics from Ireland and Germany often objected to many of the values taught in common schools, including temperance as well as the required readings and prayers from Protestant Bibles. Jews from southern and eastern Europe as well as Asians also challenged the Protestant values inherent in the common school curriculum.

In short, while the one-room common schools of the countryside and the emerging graded schools in urban centers seemed to have worked well in our relatively homogenous, early American society, they failed to meet the economic, demographic, and cultural challenges of the new nation at the turn of the twentieth century.

Pedagogy: Memorization Continues

In terms of pedagogy, teachers continued to force children to memorize facts from textbooks. As Charles Francis Adams Jr. noted in Quincy, Massachusetts, teachers "unconsciously made pupils into parrots." Children, he went on, "glibly chatter out boundaries and capitals, and principal towns and rivers of states and nations and enumerate the waters you pass through and the ports you would make in a voyage from Boston to Calcutta, or New York to Pittsburgh."

Then, in 1882, the U.S. Bureau of Education conducted a "common school studies" survey and noted that teachers continued to spend most of their classroom time requiring students to memorize facts. The study concluded that the purpose of instruction appeared to be "the guessing of so many riddles." In short, drills and recitations were more important than work that stimulated the imagination of children.

Later in the mid-1890s, J. Fitch, an English educator, came to the United States to observe the progress of our common school system. Fitch was appalled! He noted that there was still a heavy reliance on memorization: "I hear in one class the boys get up one after another reciting the names, dates, and chief performances of the eighteen presidents of the United States." Fitch also wrote that "in another school, the girls recited in order the names of principal inventors and discoverers with a description of the exploits of each."

Similarly, in 1893, Joseph Mayer Rice published his influential study of education, titled *The Public School System of the United States*. He wrote scathingly of common schools, noting that despite attempts to reform education, traditional methods of instruction and discipline persisted. Children were required to memorize materials they did not understand, and teachers resembled "Gradgrind," the notorious schoolmaster in Dickens' *Hard Times*.

The "Dead Common School Zone"

A few years later, in 1896, the editor of *The School Journal* bemoaned that "the study of pedagogy has been and still is derided by what may be termed the Three R Men. They have said and still say that it is enough to know the subjects to be taught and how to keep order." Another observer noted that a "dead common school zone" prevailed in many classrooms. The authoritarian-centered approach to education was alive and well.

Corporal Punishment

While the common school curriculum tenaciously focused on traditional curricular methods, severe corporal punishment also persisted. Benjamin Gue, an upstate New York teacher, for example, was often criticized for his more "modern" curricular and disciplinary policies. During his last year as teacher, he boarded with the Hawley family.

Mr. Hawley routinely encouraged Gue to change his teaching methods. One day Hawley complained that he "did not whip enough." Gue responded that "no scholar had refused to mind (and that he) had no occasion for whipping." In a huff, Mr. Hawley retorted that he "thought it was a good plan to whip sometimes."

Mary Augusta Roper of Templeton, Massachusetts, also received severe criticism for her progressive methods of discipline. Mary had trained at the Hartford Institute and when she graduated at the age of 19, she obtained her first teaching position at Mill Point, Michigan. She conducted her classroom as she was trained and "never used the rod unless a scholar refused to obey." Nevertheless, parents were soon in an uproar and demanded her removal because she "don't lick them at all."

NORMAL SCHOOLS FALL SHORT

Educational reformers of the early- to mid-nineteenth century certainly understood the need for improvements in education and teacher training. Both Emma Willard and Horace Mann were strong advocates of normal schools to fill the ranks of teachers in common and graded schools across the nation. And yet, despite their heroic efforts, normal schools often fell short and produced teachers who were grounded in traditional educational methods.

As Francis Parker noted in an address in Lancaster, Pennsylvania, and later published in the *Wisconsin Journal of Education*, while the country had successfully expanded the common school and the graded schools in urban centers throughout the nation, there were still major problems facing education.

Parker went on to say that American public schools needed 300,000 teachers who were skilled and trained, and that the normal school plan was a progressive step in meeting this challenge. But the aspiring teachers, while enthusiastic, were often deficient in basic skills. As a result, normal schools diverted much of their instruction to the "common branches" of education rather than progressive teacher training.

"Arrogant" Normal School Teachers

Parker also noted that many of these teachers were arrogant: "I have seen normal teachers who responded to criticism or suggestions with a smile of superiority which is so blighting to a modest man, and which told of their confidence in their ability to cover the whole ground of any given subject and put it in diagram form on the blackboard in fifteen minutes."

He went on to say that this self-confidence "simply puts a barrier between the teacher (and students) by making him believe that he knows everything." The best teachers however should have an attitude of humility—a spirit that says, "I don't know, but I want to know."

PROGRESSIVES ADDRESS THESE PROBLEMS

These and other problems of education were well understood by a handful of educational reformers at the turn of the century. Known collectively as progressives, these educators sought to transform the fundamental nature of American education. Informed by the work of such foundationalists as Johann Pestalozzi, Friedrich Froebel, John Locke, Jean-Jacques Rousseau, and others, they sought to reinvent education.

FRANCIS PARKER

Among these important progressive educators was Francis Parker, who embraced many of the ideas of these foundationalists. Born at the dawn of the common school movement in 1837, he spent his entire adult life focused on developing new approaches to education. Parker's contributions to the field of education were so important that John Dewey once called him the "father of progressive education."

Parker believed strongly in what we now refer to as the "whole child." For him, the mental, physical, and moral elements of a child should be the teacher's primary focus. He stood firmly against standardization—before it had become a major problem in education. He rejected rote learning and memorization, and favored an educational system that would encourage students to think for themselves and develop an independent approach to life.

Early Life and Teaching

Parker was born in Bedford, Hew Hampshire, and attended public schools. At the age of 16 he became a "village teacher" in Boscawen, New Hampshire, where he taught 75 students, many of whom were older than he was. This "trial by fire" seasoned young Francis, who would go on to teach at a number of schools in his late teens and early 20s.

He taught at a series of common schools in Auburn, New Hampshire, and Hinsdale, Massachusetts, and then became a "regional superintendent" of all the grammar schools in the town of Piscataquis, New Hampshire, while still in his teens. Then, at the age of 21, he traveled west, where he accepted a position as principal of a school in Carrollton, Illinois.

The Civil War

Parker's career as a teacher was interrupted by the Civil War. When the war broke out, the young 24-year-old returned to his home state of New Hampshire and enlisted as a private in the 4th New Hampshire Volunteer Infantry. Soon he was elected lieutenant and then became chief officer of the company. He rose in the ranks and, by January 1865, he had become Lieutenant Colonel and commander of his entire unit, serving in St. Augustine, Florida. Within just a month however, Francis was captured and sent to a prisoner of war camp in North Carolina until the war finally ended later that year.

From New Hampshire to Dayton

When Francis was released in May 1865, he made his way back to New Hampshire. Soon he accepted a post at Manchester, New Hampshire, where he taught for two years. However, his methods of teaching were a bit too progressive for the parochial town, and his time there was an unhappy one. Then, in 1868, he was offered a position as the principal of the First District

School in Dayton, Ohio. He happily took the job, though the journey from New Hampshire to Ohio was long and arduous.

Francis, his wife Phenie, and their daughter finally arrived in Dayton later that summer and he soon began to prepare for his new position. But he found that he had his work cut out for him. Although Dayton was a prosperous city with a population of more than 30,000, the schools had been neglected. For example, he found that only about two-thirds of the school-age children attended school.

"Colonel Parker"

The citizenry of Dayton wanted change, and were furious with the former school administration. The Republican *Dayton Journal*, for example, wrote that the schools had neglected the education of the masses. For its part, the Democrat *Daily Ledger* wrote that the "crying evil of the schools [was] the cramming process and the hot-house haste with which little children were pushed ahead in their studies."

For these reasons, there was general acceptance of Parker's new progressive approaches to education. The school board and both the Republican and Democratic newspapers hailed Parker as a fine teacher, administrator, and hero during the Civil War. Early on he was referred to as "Colonel Parker" or "The Colonel," and the name stuck for the rest of his life.

Parker's new school enrolled nearly 700 students, 400 of whom ranged from 6 to 10 years of age. He accepted the challenge even though he admitted that he knew very little about teaching younger children. Parker soon found that his teaching staff also had little training in this area.

Dayton's Traditional Pedagogy

The typical curricular approach in this and other schools in Dayton was based on what was referred to as the "examination system." Students were assessed on the basis of the number of words they had memorized or math problems they had solved, with "grades" also given for attendance and deportment.

On examination days, Parker wrote, communities "went wild" telegraphing each other, bragging of the high scores of their students. Parker continued this system of "memorization and examination" for a time but gradually introduced new approaches, including the "word" method (look–say, where students were taught the whole word rather than just its phonetic components).

Dayton Normal School

In 1869, with the support of Parker, the Dayton School Board recommended that a newly completed school become a normal school with a year-long curriculum combining theory and actual practice. Qualified female residents of Dayton could attend the new school free of charge if they agreed to teach for two years in the local school system. Women who were nonresidents were charged a nominal fee of $60. Colonel Parker was selected as the principal of this new institution. He recruited new teachers and launched a new curriculum for the school.

University of Berlin

Despite achieving success as the head of the Sixth District School and as principal of the newly established Dayton Normal School, Colonel Parker departed the city in 1872. Inconsolable over the death of his wife Phenie and his young daughter, he was determined to set a new course for his life and career and study education in Europe. His long journey to Europe culminated in Berlin, where he was admitted to the distinguished Humboldt University.

Parker enrolled in what we now might call a "nontraditional" curriculum of his own choosing. He studied psychology, history, philosophy, and pedagogies. School administrators, however, warned him that his choice of courses would not lead to a degree—to which Parker said, "but they do lead to the children of America."

Introduction to European Masters

Parker studied with the distinguished Professor Friedrich Harms, who had been a student of Hegel. Harms believed that philosophers should turn to the understanding of education that he saw as the greatest of all human endeavors. Harms also directed Parker's interest to the study of the great European masters including Pestalozzi, Froebel, Rousseau, and Herbart.

Parker embraced these new ideas and was especially interested in Froebel's "child gardening movement." He even visited the widowed Frau Froebel's kindergarten in Berlin. Through these experiences and his extensive reading of Pestalozzi, he gained a deeper understanding of "object teaching," noting later that instructors must present objects to reference the child's "mental sight."

Integrating German Methods with American Democracy

While Parker learned a great deal in Berlin, he also understood that while the German methods of instruction were often superior to those in the United States, the rigid authoritarian structure of the schools themselves was misdirected. He came to believe that the common school, with its democratic basis and coeducational framework, was the more appropriate form of school organization in the United States.

Parker's goal, then, was to integrate the best of German pedagogy into the structure of American education. After two years abroad, Parker returned to the United States in the winter of 1875 brimming with new ideas and idealistic resolve.

Superintendent of Schools in Quincy

Colonel Parker had some difficulty obtaining a supervisory or teaching position in the late winter of 1875. The economic depression that began in 1873 continued to plague the United States and the labor market in general. Parker then noticed an advertisement for a superintendent of schools in Quincy, Massachusetts. His application was received on April 7, 1875, and the Quincy Board of Education unanimously agreed to hire him beginning in just weeks. Parker packed his bags and arrived in Quincy just in the nick of time, on April 20.

When he reached Quincy, the temperature was 25 degrees, but the entire School Committee greeted him enthusiastically at the train station. Parker immediately went to work with the committee's request for "gradual remodeling" of the school system, but was warned that reorganization would take time.

Colonel Parker was put in charge of seven schools in Quincy that included 1,600 students in the primary, intermediate, and grammar school grades as well as high school. He met with teachers the day after his arrival and then proceeded to visit each of the seven schools accompanied by Charles Adams, grandson of John Quincy Adams.

Quincy Schools: "Wearisome"

Although Adams described the day with Parker as "useful and happy," Parker was appalled by the fact that by the time that children came to school, their natural curiosity and need for activity was destroyed by "dull, wearisome hours of listless activities upon hard benches."

In fact, his first report to the School Committee noted that the love for school was often crushed out of the "little innocents." He went on to say that the benches at the schools seemed to be "invented to torture the little ones." Later he wrote that there was a mechanical nature to learning at the schools, with students parroting words without understanding their meaning. Indeed, one of his first priorities was to help teachers understand that "words in themselves have (no) mysterious power of creating ideas," or promoting learning.

"A Stagecoach of Educational Methods"

He summarized his concerns for the Quincy schools (and schools in general) when he wrote that despite the dramatic economic and technological growth of the nation as a whole, schools across the nation were still moving in the "stagecoach of educational methods." As a result, Parker proclaimed early in his tenure at Quincy that his job as superintendent was to become a "teacher of teachers." This would be accomplished through a collaboration among teachers by meeting together and sharing ideas and problems.

The Quincy Method Takes Shape

By the end of his first year as superintendent of schools in Quincy, the contours of what would become known as the "Quincy Method" began to take shape. The elements of the Quincy Methods were clear.

Rejection of Memorization

First, Parker rejected memorization and recitation. He also demanded an end to the rigid school routine and what he called the "spelling book" method. He reportedly said that all spelling books "should be burned."

Social Skills, Collaboration, and Self-Expression

Secondly, he insisted that there must be an emphasis on the social skills of communication and collaboration with others. Third, he emphasized the need for students to develop a sense of self-expression through cultural activities, physical education, experience-based learning and student writing.

The "Object Method"

Fourth, he promoted the "object method" as envisioned by Pestalozzi. He felt strongly that showing and talking about an object with young students must precede giving it an abstract name. Fifth, Parker felt that reading for primary students must be approached through the word method, sometimes called the "look–say" method, augmented with phonics.

"A Pleasant, Cheerful Home"

In short, Parker believed that the first years of school must be like a "pleasant, cheerful home (where the) little folks play, sing, read, count objects, write, draw and are happy under the direction of very faithful and efficient teachers."

The Quincy Method was a great success. By the end of the 1870s, the Massachusetts State Board of Education published a survey demonstrating that Quincy students excelled at reading, writing, and spelling and performed very well in math. Soon, visitors from throughout the country flocked to Quincy to study what was now referred to as the "Quincy System." Moreover, Quincy teachers were recruited to teach at other schools and, as a result, they spread these new progressive methods throughout the nation.

Praise for Parker's System and National Celebrity

Later, Lelia E. Partridge marveled at the success of the Quincy schools in her book, *The Quincy Methods Illustrated.* She wrote that in the Quincy schools "the child was the objective point and not the courses of study, examinations or promotions." The Quincy Method, moreover, was built on "comradeship of teacher and pupils . . . (in an atmosphere) of happy work."

By 1881, Colonel Parker had become a national celebrity. But after six years in Quincy, he reluctantly left his position and traveled to Boston, where he became the supervisor of 42 primary schools in eight school districts with more than 50,000 students and 400 teachers.

Miss Stuart

Although Parker felt he needed a rest from his grueling supervisory duties, he agreed to give a series of lectures at the Martha's Vineyard Summer Institute in 1881. There he met Frances Stuart from the Boston School of Oratory. Miss Stuart, as Parker called her, was 10 years his junior, a women's rights activist, and a strong advocate of progressive educational methods. By the end of the institute Parker and "Miss Stuart" had become close friends. The two scholars eventually married in November 1882.

"The Colonel" Moves to Chicago

It was during this time that Parker was recruited to become the principal of the Cook County Normal School. He enjoyed his short time in Boston, but felt that the political infighting in the city represented a danger to his career. He and Miss Stuart packed their bags and moved to Cook County, just outside the Chicago city limits.

Parker spent the next 20 years in and around Chicago and established an innovative school that would eventually merge with John Dewey's Lab School at the University of Chicago in 1901. His successes in Chicago, Boston, and Quincy had made him a legend among educators and, as we have seen, prompted Dewey to call him "the father of progressive education." "The Colonel" passed in 1902, but his legacy of collaboration and progressive, child-centered teaching would continue.

COLLABORATION WITH DEWEY

The collaboration between Francis Parker and John Dewey was strong and direct. Both were driven by a belief in the importance of child-centered learning, and the two were colleagues at the University of Chicago when Parker's Chicago Institute merged with Dewey's Lab School to create the University Elementary School in 1901. Their direct personal connection, however, was short because of Parker's declining health. Parker's passing in 1902 was followed by Dewey's departure for Columbia University in 1904.

Nevertheless, the intellectual roots of both men were similarly focused on such figures as John Locke, Jean-Jacques Rousseau, and Johann Pestalozzi. And of course, as we have seen, John Dewey had a great deal of respect and admiration for "the Colonel."

JOHN DEWEY

And yet, despite his deference to Parker, their close personal connections and collaborative efforts, John Dewey clearly was the "Dean of Progressive Education." His academic work, rooted in psychology and pedagogical theory, represented a fundamental turning point in education and spawned generations of child-centered progressive educators and schools.

Early Life

John Dewey was born in Burlington, Vermont, on October 20, 1859. He grew up in a middle-class home, had access to books, and enjoyed the intellectual stimulation of his parents, especially his father, Archibald. John attended public schools and at the age of 15 was accepted as a student at the University of Vermont where he excelled, graduating second in his class at the age of 19.

Johns Hopkins

Dewey then became a teacher, but struggled in the classroom. After three years of teaching in Pennsylvania and Vermont, he realized that teaching in the common school was not his strength. He applied to graduate school and was accepted at Johns Hopkins University in 1882. He was 22 years old. It was at Johns Hopkins that his real intellectual journey began. He studied philosophy with the renowned professor, G. Stanley Hall, and earned his PhD two years later at the age of 24, writing his dissertation on Immanuel Kant.

Although Dewey developed quickly under the direction of his mentor Hall, the two gradually parted ways. Hall had become fascinated with an emerging field of eugenics and eventually embraced the use of both questionnaires and then standardized tests to determine students' IQs. Although the early use of standardized tests had been diagnostic in nature, designed to identify students with learning problems, Hall used these data to sort individuals into academic tracks based on their examination performance.

A Schism with His Mentor

Dewey was uneasy with this use of testing. He did not reject the "assessment" of student progress, but he favored a diagnostic approach to help students who were having learning difficulties. In fact, Dewey came to believe that all children could learn given the correct environment and methods of instruction. Here we see his democratic and progressive educational philosophy beginning to develop while he was still a graduate student and during his early years as an academic.

The schism between Hall and Dewey in some ways is reflected in education today. The more authoritarian, teacher-centered approach of Hall featured standardized testing, curriculum tracking and, years later in the twenty-first century, would emerge as a conservative legislative fiat known as "no child left behind." Dewey, on the other hand, came to favor a more democratic, child-centered approach to education.

University of Michigan: A Shift from Philosophy to Education

Following graduate school, Dewey took a position in the Department of Psychology at the University of Michigan. In 1886, he published his important text, *Psychology*, and three years later he moved intellectually to the field of education with his *Applied Psychology: Introduction to the Principles and Practice of Education*.

Beginning with his *Applied Psychology* and then other works throughout his career, Dewey drew insights from psychology and integrated them into the emerging field of education. His work on the philosophy of experience, for example, informed his understanding of how children learn and formed the basis of experiential education, a core element of his emerging pedagogy.

Similarly, his early work on democracy as a psychology student gave him an understanding of its importance in education. Dewey wrote that "democracy is the one, ultimate ethical ideal of humanity." This became the foundation of his seminal ideas in *Democracy and Education*, published in 1916.

University of Chicago and the Lab School

Dewey's philosophy of education continued to develop during his years at Michigan, and, in 1892, he was personally invited by President William Rainey Harper to join the faculty at the University of Chicago. After considerable negotiations, he accepted the position and moved to Chicago in 1894. Central to his acceptance was the promise of a laboratory school on campus. Dewey worked with Harper for the next several months, and the Lab School opened in January 1896.

Although the school had rather modest beginnings with only 12 students and one teacher, it had great promise. Within five years the school had grown to an enrollment of 140 students, 23 teachers, and 10 graduate student assistants.

Both John and his wife, Alice Chipman Dewey, were pleased with this innovative experiment in education. The school represented a joyful period of learning, with a child-centered focus that rejected the traditional curriculum of the day.

The "Four Basic Interests of Children"

Dewey's Lab School integrated what he called the "four basic interests of children." These interests, he argued, provided the curricular foundation of the school itself and included: communicating and discussing, making and building objects, exploring and investigation, and artistic expression.

In addition, Dewey built on the work of Rousseau, Pestalozzi, and Froebel, and developed a curriculum that centered on the curiosity and experiences of students. This child-centered approach, he noted, would help students learn naturally through their own experiences.

"Learning by Doing"

The final elements of Dewey's Lab School curriculum focused on "learning by doing" (experiential learning) and a "problem solving" approach. Dewey noted that students did not learn when things were presented in an abstract, top-down manner. But by experiencing a game, a process, a discussion, or an experiment, they would remain engaged and learn. Similarly, by drawing on students' innate interest in discovery and exploration, Dewey emphasized the "problem solving" approach to learning.

Collaborative Problem Solving

A good example of how Dewey constructed the curriculum was his emphasis on solving contemporary problems in the classroom for the common good. Here the use of problem-solving approaches and group collaborations worked well.

Dewey argued that individualism had essentially replaced our sense of community. As a result, students had difficulty understanding the interdependency of our social, political, and economic order. But through these collaborative problem-solving skills, students would be better prepared for a life of social service and community involvement.

Finally, in addition to these core curricular approaches, Dewey also embraced several other innovative pedagogical elements for the Lab School. These included a rejection of textbooks in favor of an integrated curriculum based on a variety of sources (similar to whole language today), group work and collaboration rather than competitive examinations, understanding rather than memorization, as well as a focus on social responsibility and service to the community.

A Brief Success

The first years of the Lab School indeed were a "joyful experiment" for both teachers and students. Dewey saw the school as an "embryonic democracy," where students had a degree of intellectual freedom and worked with teachers to shape the curriculum and instruction. Teachers had greater autonomy and fewer administrative duties. Moreover, the classroom had a more relaxed atmosphere, with engaged students less likely to be disruptive and cause disciplinary problems.

Criticism of the Lab School

But soon, the school's curriculum, its teachers, and its leadership came under fire. Lab School classrooms were often loud as children expressed themselves and worked together. This did not sit well with administrators and especially parents. Moreover, some Lab School teachers found that the problem-solving component of the curriculum was difficult for them and their students. Many reverted to teacher-centered approaches to deal with these curricular difficulties.

As a result, the Lab School slowly changed. First, specialized teachers were replaced with more "general education" instructors. Then, classrooms gradually became graded, and administrators gained more control over the day-to-day activities of teachers and students. Finally, the school abandoned its democratically structured curriculum and adopted a standardized "Outline of Course of Study."

Nevertheless, Dewey maintained his belief that the child-centered approach to education was superior to what he called the subject-centered, teacher-centered curriculum. He published these ideas in his *The Child and the Curriculum* in 1902. While he celebrated this approach, he did note that there were flaws in child-centered learning, which sometimes tended to overlook the importance of the teacher and ignored the basics. Nevertheless, he maintained his support for child-centered learning.

Dangers of Teacher-Centered Instruction

As a result, Dewey recommended a synthesis of child- and teacher-centered approaches to education. And yet, he warned educators that too much reliance on teacher-centered instruction was dangerous. It encouraged passivity, stifled creativity, and developed students who were more compliant with authoritarianism. This, of course, is a valuable lesson for today.

Departure from the School

When Parker's Chicago Institute merged with the Lab School in 1901, the balance of power at the institution changed dramatically. Institute teachers now represented more than 70 percent of the faculty at the school, and there was a growing chorus of criticism of Alice Chipman Dewey's administrative capabilities. John Dewey attempted to resolve the problems but was unsuccessful. Frustrated and angry, he and Alice left the school in 1903, and John took a position at Columbia University in New York.

John Dewey's Legacy

John Dewey would continue to write, lecture, and teach for many years. The work that he and Alice Chipman Dewey did with the Lab School and the brilliant legacy of John's curricular ideas and theory presented in hundreds of articles and books have inspired generations of educators and spawned what we know as the progressive education movement.

Many progressive schools employed a model similar to the Lab School. These included Marietta Johnson's Fairhope School, the Lincoln School of Teachers College, the Park School of Baltimore, New Jersey's Modern School, Margaret Naumberg's Walden School, and the more radical Manumit School that was organized around the model of labor unions. These and many others were inspired by the work of John Dewey, either directly or indirectly.

THE RISE, FALL, AND REBIRTH OF PROGRESSIVE EDUCATION

The efforts of the progressive education movement reached its peak during the 1930s, but by the 1950s a wave of conservativism associated with the Cold War and virulent anti-intellectualism limited its influence. Schools often reverted to a more standardized curriculum, with teacher-centered pedagogy, vocational training and, of course, the growing power of school administrators.

Despite this setback, progressive education experienced a revival in the 1960s as a new generation of educators sought a return to the ideals of Dewey and the child-centered approach to education. These ideas were linked to a growing interest in desegregation, inclusion, and early educational opportunities for the poor.

In addition, this period inspired a host of new curricular ideas reminiscent of the early progressives, especially John Dewey. Among the best known of these innovations were inquiry-based instruction, individual contracting, flexible scheduling, team teaching, and the open classroom. There also was a revival of sorts that emphasized collaboration and cooperation rather than competition in the classroom. Clearly the spirit of John Dewey, the real "father of progressive education," had a lasting impact on American education.

MARIA MONTESSORI

As we have seen, there was a clear international dimension to the development of education. The work of foundationalists such as Jean-Jacques Rousseau, John Locke, Friedrich Frobel, Johann Pestalozzi, and Voltaire informed educators throughout the early nineteenth century and had a dramatic impact on progressive educators at the end of the nineteenth and into the twentieth centuries.

Less well known during this period but one of the towering figures in education today was Italian-born Maria Montessori. Because of her gender, foreign birth, cohabitation with her lover outside of marriage, and her illegitimate son that she all but abandoned until he was in his teens, Montessori was a kind of pariah in the world educational community. Nevertheless, this courageous woman continued her pioneering work and today there are more than 20,000 schools throughout the world bearing her name, with more than 3,000 in the United States alone.

Early Life

Maria Montessori was born on August 31, 1870, in Chiaravalle, Italy. Both her father and mother had distinguished professional careers and her mother encouraged Maria to continue her education. Maria was an exceptionally bright young women and had aspirations beyond the proscribed roles for women in the nineteenth century.

She attended public school beginning at age six, and then at 13 she enrolled at the Regia Scuola Tecnica Michelangelo Buonarroti, an all-boys technical school, with the intention of becoming an engineer. Maria soon changed her career focus, however, and decided to become a physician. She excelled in her pre-med studies and entered the medical program at Sapienza University in Rome.

Medical School

As the first woman to attend medical school at the university, she encountered enormous obstacles including harassment from some of her classmates and professors. For example, because of her gender, she was not allowed to dissect cadavers in the presence of men and was forced to do her work at night alone. Nevertheless, she pressed on, and graduated with honors in 1896, at the age of 26.

During her medical career Maria studied pediatrics and psychiatry and was exposed to the plight of children with physical and mental disabilities in state hospitals and orphanages. When she graduated, she turned her attention to the suffering of these children. Soon she was conducting research on children with cognitive and physical disabilities. She lectured widely and gained a reputation as a both an advocate for disabled children and women's rights.

Disabled Children

Meanwhile, Maria developed the basics of her system of education that she would later call her "scientific pedagogy." She was inspired by two French physicians, Jean Marc Gaspard Itard and Edouard Seguin, both of whom worked with children with intellectual disabilities. Itard was the first to identify Tourette's syndrome, while Seguin had established a school for deaf children and those with intellectual deficiencies.

A Return to the Educational Foundationalists

Their work inspired Montessori, and she turned from clinical work and private practice in medicine to education. She audited a number of university courses and it's been reported that she read "all the major works on educational theory of the past two hundred years." These included works by Rousseau, Pestalozzi, Froebel, and many others.

Orthophrenic School

This work strengthened her resolve to help the unfortunate children who had mental disabilities. In 1900, under the auspices of the National League for the Protection of Retarded Children, she helped to establish the Orthophrenic School to train teachers to educate mentally disabled children. During her two-year tenure as co-director of the school, she trained hundreds of teachers using methods that she had developed. Later Maria would adapt these methods for all children.

Not satisfied with her educational background, Maria returned to the University of Rome for more education. There she spent the next two years immersing herself in a variety of subjects including educational philosophy, psychology, and anthropology. She also published widely about disabled children.

Casa dei Bambini (Children's House)

In 1906, Montessori took a position to oversee the education of poor children living in an apartment complex in the San Lorenzo district of Rome. Here she applied her pedagogical methods, originally designed for the disabled, to the children. One of her colleagues suggested she call the project the *Casa dei Bambini* or Children's House—and it stuck. The first of these Casas opened in January 1907 and enrolled 60 children in the early primary grades.

The initial curriculum was simple and basic. She focused on children's personal care including, washing, combing their hair, dressing, and undressing. Students also were instructed to care for the environment by cleaning the classroom and tending the garden outside the school. Montessori did not teach the children directly but carefully observed their day-to-day activities.

Montessori observed that the children were more interested in practical matters and, to her surprise, were not motivated by rewards such as sweets or food. As a result, she altered her instruction to include even more useful activities such as cooking, gymnastics, and the care of pets. She then altered the classroom environment itself, replacing unused heavy furniture with child-size tables and chairs that could easily be moved by the children themselves. Moreover, shelves were installed that were low enough so that small children could reach materials on them.

This new environment and practical curriculum also led to what Montessori called "spontaneous discipline." Children intuitively understood that this new environment was their own and, as a result, they treated it with respect and dignity.

The success of the Children's Houses led to the opening of another school in 1907. Here, Montessori expanded the curriculum to reading and writing using the idea of learning through the senses. This technique was reminiscent of Pestalozzi's Gertrude. She cut out letters of the alphabet from sandpaper that children could touch. Soon, many had become proficient in both reading and writing. Gradually her success came to the attention of other educators, politicians, and journalists, and her reputation spread rapidly.

From her work in the Children's Houses, Montessori understood that children learned best by manipulating objects in an open classroom setting. Following the lead of Rousseau, Montessori noted that when children were allowed to choose activities that they were interested in, they learned much more quickly and effectively.

"Peer Teaching"

Perhaps because of her reading of Lancaster, Maria Montessori also recognized the importance of what we now refer to as peer teaching and collaborative learning. She placed students in multi-age groups based on a three-year span, recognizing that children of different ages can help each other learn. She wrote that while the teacher might have difficulty explaining certain concepts such as sharing to a three-year-old, a five-year-old could communicate the idea "with the utmost ease."

Based on her success in the Children's Houses in the next few years, Maria published her classic treatise on teaching in 1909, entitled *The Montessori Method: Scientific Pedagogy as Applied to Child Education in "The Children's Houses."* This important work introduced the Montessori method to an international audience, including many progressive educators in this country.

Growth and Criticism of the Casa

By 1912, Montessori schools had been officially established throughout Italy, Switzerland, and Paris, with others planned in countries throughout the world. In the United States, a number of Montessori schools were established, and, by 1913, more than 100 such schools had opened.

Despite her success, however, there were a number of critics of her methods. William Heard Kilpatrick, for example, dismissed the Montessori method in his book *The Montessori Method Examined*, while the National Kindergarten Association and others argued that her methods were outdated and too rigid, with too much reliance on sense training, leaving little time for creative activities and play.

Others were critical of Montessori's tight control over the curriculum that she had developed. As a result, the momentum of growth of her schools in the United States slowed until after her death in 1951, when there was a renaissance of her methods.

Despite the criticism that she received in the United States, the Montessori method of teaching and her reputation continued to grow during this period. Montessori schools were established throughout Europe, and later in India.

Difficulties in the 1930s and during World War II

Montessori and her family had great difficulties both in Italy and abroad during the 1930s and throughout World War II. In Italy, she and her son Mario came under surveillance by the Fascist government of Benito Mussolini because of her peace activism. As a result, she fled Italy to the Netherlands in the early 1930s. Moreover, during the war, she was often scrutinized and detained as a foreign national of an enemy nation.

Postwar Success

And yet, following the war, Montessori reestablished her reputation and continued her advocacy of children. She was actively involved in the United

Nations Educational, Scientific, and Cultural Organisation (UNESCO) and played a primary role in establishing its Institute for Education in 1951. Montessori was nominated for the Nobel Peace Prize three times, received the French Legion of Honor for her continuing peace efforts following the war, and received an honorary doctorate from the University of Amsterdam.

The Spirit of Progressive Education

Maria Montessori passed from this world quite suddenly in December 1951. Nevertheless, her advocacy for children, whom she referred to as the "forgotten citizens" of the world, as well as her determined efforts for peace were important contributions. Moreover, her progressive spirit and intellectual collaboration with the educational foundationalists of the eighteenth and nineteenth centuries places her at the heart of the progressive child-centered movement of the twentieth century and beyond.

The spirit of progressive education has endured a great deal of criticism throughout the years. Its child-centered focus, its unstructured learning environment, and its innovative methods often "struck a nerve" with more traditional "authoritarian" educators and administrators.

Nevertheless, from the eighteenth-century work of Rousseau and Voltaire and its application by nineteenth-century figures such as Pestalozzi and Froebel, through the work of progressive educators such as Parker, Dewey, and Montessori, this spirit has survived and thrived. Moreover, elements of critical pedagogy and neoprogressive schools carry on those traditions and maintain the ideas of child-centered learning today.

Chapter 9

Champions of Racial Justice

As we have seen, the brief period of hope for racial justice and equality in education for African American children during the early years of Reconstruction was crushed by a growing wave of white nationalism and racism in the form of the "redeemers" movement in the late 1870s. When Reconstruction ended in 1877 as a result of the infamous "Compromise of 1877," the hopes and dreams of millions of former slaves were shattered.

Freedmen Bureau schools were closed, defunded, or burned by such vigilante groups as the Ku Klux Klan. Black and white teachers were threatened and intimidated, and many simply returned to their former lives in both the North and the South. The Jubilee seemed to be over.

THE STRUGGLE FOR EDUCATION DURING JIM CROW

Nevertheless, the quest for racial justice on the one hand, and the education of young African American children on the other, would punctuate the Jim Crow years. A number of black colleges were established throughout the South including Atlanta University, Howard University, Morehouse College, Scotia Seminary, and Spelman College for women.

TUSKEGEE

And while these and other black institutions would form the basis of the 107 historically black colleges today, it was Tuskegee University founded in 1881 that established the important collaboration between philanthropists and the African American educational community.

As we have seen, when Booker T. Washington became the president of Tuskegee in 1882, he not only nurtured a school that would provide students with occupational skills that would help them to survive in Jim Crow America,

Figure 9.1. Winning the *Brown v. Board of Education* decision: George E. C. Hayes, Thurgood Marshall, and James Nabrit, 1954. Staff photographer, *New York World Telegram*. https://commons.wikimedia.org/wiki/File:George_Edward_Chalmer_Hayes,_Thurgood_Marshall,_and_James_Nabrit_in_1954_winning_Brown_case.jpg.

but also reached out to white philanthropists to support his educational vision. Washington and his wife, Olivia America Davidson, sought funding and collaboration with wealthy gilded age industrialists and businessmen.

The Washingtons' success provided a model for late-nineteenth- and early-twentieth-century African American education that essentially rejected the traditional classical curriculum of the university in favor of one that was more vocationally oriented. It was this approach that appealed to white progressive businessmen and many African Americans desperate to support their families. But not everyone was happy with this direction in education.

A NEW GENERATION OF ACTIVISTS

A new generation of black activists, born in the depths of Jim Crow, had a different perspective on racial justice. They rejected accommodation to the dominate white society. Among these were W. E. B. Du Bois, Horace Mann Bond, Charles Hamilton Houston, and Thurgood Marshall.

W. E. B. DU BOIS

William Edward Burghardt Du Bois was born on February 23, 1868, at the beginning of the Reconstruction period. He grew up in Great Barington, Massachusetts, and was sheltered from the violence and lynching of the Jim Crow South. His father left him and his mother when he was just two years old. Then when he was 12, William's mother had a major stroke that disabled her for the rest of her life. She died five years later in 1885.

Du Bois's Early Life

Despite these traumatic experiences, young William grew up in the warm and loving embrace of his grandparents and other members of his extended family. He attended public school in the nearly all-white community and, like most of his classmates, was on track to go to college. And that is what Du Bois did. In 1885, at the age of 18, he left Great Barrington and traveled to Nashville to attend Fisk University.

Jim Crow, Firsthand

In Nashville, Du Bois experienced the disenfranchisement, violence, lynching, and bigotry of the Jim Crow South for the first time. These experiences had a profound effect on the young man. He graduated from Fisk in three years, and, in 1888, he was accepted to Harvard University. However, there was one major stipulation: Harvard would not accept his degree nor any of the credits he had earned at Fisk.

Disappointed but determined, Du Bois enrolled at Harvard and soon began his studies under the renowned scholar William James. He applied himself and completed his bachelor's degree in history in just two years. Because of his distinguished work as an undergraduate, he was offered a postgraduate scholarship at Harvard to continue his education, but instead accepted a fellowship from the Slater fund to study at the University of Berlin.

Berlin

Du Bois's work at the University of Berlin as well as his experiences traveling throughout Europe during this period had a profound impact on the young man. There he made many new friends and was introduced to a number of influential scholars, including Gustav Schmoller and Heinrich von Treitschke.

When Du Bois reflected on these experiences later in his life, he recalled, "I found myself on the outside of the American world looking in. With me were white folk—students, acquaintances, teachers—who viewed the scene with me. They did not pause to regard me as a curiosity . . . I was just a man."

Wilberforce College

Du Bois returned to Harvard and completed his PhD in history in 1895. He was 28 years old. He then accepted a position as an assistant professor at Wilberforce College in Ohio, where he taught for a number of years. During this period, two major events would change the trajectory of his career and his life. The first was his marriage to one of his former students at Wilberforce College, Nina Gormer, and the second was his summer fellowship from the University of Pennsylvania that allowed him to study a black community in Philadelphia.

The Philadelphia Negro

The results of this research led to the publication of *The Philadelphia Negro* in 1899. This work reassessed the prevailing negative image of black people in that community. Du Bois noted that there were some major problems facing blacks in Philadelphia, including poverty, crime, and illiteracy. But rather than perceiving these problems as inherent to the black experience, he argued that they were due to racism and a lack of education. This led to fewer economic opportunities, poverty, despair, and crime.

Talented Tenth

Du Bois argued that black communities possessed their own internal class structure and economic organization that was often ignored by scholars. Typically, black communities were judged based on what he called the "submerged tenth"—the poor, the undereducated, and the unemployed. But Du Bois wrote that there was another important group of blacks that he later referred to as the "talented tenth": individuals who had education, professional careers, and were leaders of their communities.

The Philadelphia Negro was the first sociological study of a black community and brought attention to Du Bois's growing body of scholarly work. It represented a major turning point in his career as a scholar and activist. During this period, he began to formulate what he would call "the Negro problem" in America.

The "Negro Problem"

This "problem" was that, while white America would only begin to appreciate the talents and contributions of black people if they were integrated into white society, blacks themselves must begin to appreciate their own unique history, heritage, experiences, and culture.

Du Bois argued that this "double consciousness" would help to sustain African Americans in the future as they contributed to white culture on the one hand and maintained their own identity on the other. He wrote that "the destiny of the race (would lead) neither to assimilation nor separatism but to proud enduring hyphenation."

Education and the "Double Consciousness"

It was at this point in his life that Du Bois recognized the central importance of education for the development of African American "double consciousness." Classical education, Du Bois argued, would provide black children the chance to excel and compete within the white-dominated society. Moreover, through education, these children would also understand their place in the important culture of the black community.

"Politics of Accommodation"

Meanwhile, the success of Tuskegee University and Booker T. Washington's "politics of accommodation" continued to dominate the thinking of some black educators, philanthropists, and the white business community in general. In his classic *Up from Slavery* published in 1901, Washington defended his vocational approach to education while rejecting classical education for African American children.

Washington wrote that a traditional classical education would give black children promises that could not be fulfilled. To make his point, he presented an apocryphal story of a young man who had just graduated from high school "sitting down in a one room cabin with grease on his clothing, filth all around him and weeds in the yard and garden engaged in studying French grammar." For Washington, vocational training was the future of African American education.

Atlanta Compromise Speech

Earlier, Washington had articulated his vision of vocational education for blacks in his famous Atlanta Compromise speech of 1895. In his address to an all-white audience attending the Cotton States and International Exposition that day, he assured them that African Americans were ready and able to assist in the development of the southern economy.

His famous statement, "cast down your bucket where you are," thrilled the attendees. He went on to say that "without strikes and labor wars [those who had] tilled your fields, cleared your forests, built your railroads and cities and brought forth treasures . . . from the earth" were now ready to help the South prosper again.

And as a tacit warning to those African Americans who may not have supported vocational training, he said "the greatest danger [for black people] in the great leap from slavery to freedom was that they may overlook the fact that they shall prosper . . . as they learn to dignify and glorify common labor and put brains and skill to the common occupations of life."

He concluded by saying that "no race can prosper until it learns that there is as much dignity in tilling a field as in writing a poem. It is at the bottom of life we must begin and not at the top. Nor should we permit our grievances to overshadow our opportunities."

Response to Atlanta Compromise Speech

Although Washington's "cast down your buckets" metaphor resonated with the assembled audience in Atlanta that September day, it triggered a growing outrage among many black civil rights leaders. Among the most vocal critics of Washington was Du Bois. While Du Bois did not reject vocational training for African American children as such, he was opposed to a sort of blanket assessment of young blacks that routinely tracked them into this sort of curriculum.

Moreover, Du Bois was furious with what he called the "scraps of education" that were given to black children by philanthropic organizations that supported Washington's accommodationist, vocational education approach. In his *The Souls of Black Folk*, published in 1903, Du Bois expanded these ideas and sharpened his arguments against Washington's educational ideas.

The Souls of Black Folk

In this classic work, Du Bois referred to Washington's "Atlanta Compromise" as the "gospel of work and money." For him, this compromise was an obvious attempt to gain the support of wealthy white donors to Tuskegee. Du Bois was so angry that he referred to Washington as "the most distinguished southerner since Jefferson Davis, the president of the Confederate States of America."

Du Bois went on to criticize Washington's educational policies as a "devil's pact" between wealthy white southerners and blacks who would guarantee their cheap labor to rebuild the South in return for free "industrial" education. This "old attitude of adjustment and submission," he went on to say, would deprive black people of political power, civil rights, and higher education for Negro youth.

He concluded his criticism of Washington's educational policies by noting that blacks were indeed ready and willing to follow the self-help and personal thrift ideas of the "Wizard of Tuskegee" but would not abide by his "apologies of injustice" that "opposes the higher training and ambition of our brighter minds."

By the early twentieth century, during a period that historians such as John Hope Franklin refer to as the nadir of "the Negro's status in American society," Du Bois had taken a stand not only for racial justice but for equity in education. This stand would now bring education into the mainstream of the growing civil rights movement of the twentieth century.

"The Problem of the Twentieth Century"

Du Bois's famous declaration that the "the problem of the twentieth century is the problem of the color line" would alert Americans that only through equal educational opportunities could the color line be crossed. It emboldened both the leadership as well as the rank and file of the civil rights movement to press for desegregated schools, full funding for black education, and open admission to universities, medical schools, and law schools for African Americans.

Du Bois's Distinguished Career

Du Bois went on to have a distinguished career as a leader of the burgeoning civil rights movement in both this country and abroad. He was one of the founders of the Niagara movement and later the National Association for the Advancement of Colored People (NAACP), where he became the influential editor of that organization's primary publication, *The Crisis*. He also recognized the pressing need to end policies of global imperialism and helped to draft the "Address to the Nations of the World." This document called upon European leaders to abandon their destructive policies of imperial expansion.

Du Bois's Collaboration

Du Bois's collaboration with hundreds of civil rights activists including Horace Mann Bond, Charles Hamilton Huston, and Thurgood Marshall would help to include educational equality for African Americans as a central element of the civil rights movement. This was one of his lasting legacies.

Moreover, his editorship of *The Crisis* shaped the direction of the NAACP during its early years, and his leadership and collaboration introduced scholars and activists to this important publication. By 1920, *The Crisis* had a readership of more than 100,000. In addition to promoting racial justice and equal educational opportunities, *The Crisis* promoted women's rights, union rights, and even interracial marriage.

HORACE MANN BOND

As editor of *The Crisis*, Du Bois helped launch the careers of a number of young scholars and activists. One of his notable proteges was Horace Mann Bond. In 1924, while still a graduate student at the University of Chicago, Bond would challenge one of the emerging and wildly popular elements of modern American education—the standardized test. With this challenge, Bond criticized what he saw as both the inherent racism of these exams as well as the dark elements of eugenics that provided their foundation.

Bond's Early Life

Horace Mann Bond was born into a middle-class black family in Nashville, Tennessee, on November 8, 1904. Both his parents were well educated. His father (James Bond!) studied at Oberlin College where he earned his doctorate in theology. His mother (Alice Brown) also studied at Oberlin, where she received her bachelor's degree in education.

Young Horace benefited from the encouragement and teaching from his mother and the religious values he derived from his father. This intellectual background led him to a career as an educator and activist for racial equality.

Horace was a precocious child. He attended public schools and graduated from high school at the age of 14. He then enrolled at Lincoln University where he graduated with a bachelor of arts in history at the age of 19. Horace then traveled north to the University of Chicago, where he earned his master's degree in 1926 and his doctorate in 1936.

Intellectual Growth

While he was a student at the University of Chicago, Horace recognized the growing social problems that were emerging not only in the United States but throughout the world. World War I had left deep scars on society, and there were powerful elements of eugenics, anti-Semitism, xenophobia, and racism emerging throughout the world.

Anti-Semitism was becoming a major problem in Europe, energized by right-wing populist leaders such as Adolph Hitler and Benito Mussolini. These and other political figures used the latent hatred of Jews to appease their base and promote their twisted political agendas. These problems would fester for another decade and eventually lead to World War II and the Holocaust.

National Origins Acts

In the United States, a new, virulent strain of racism in the form of the Ku Klux Klan spread beyond the South, built on racism, anti-Catholicism, and anti-immigration. Moving in lockstep with these dark elements, conservative Republicans passed a series of anti-immigrant laws collectively known as the National Origins Acts, which dramatically restricted immigration to this country.

Eugenics

Young Horace Bond intuitively understood that at the heart of this new and dangerous political environment was eugenics. Eugenics had developed in the last quarter of the nineteenth century and was a perversion of Darwinian evolutionary theory.

Darwin, of course, had theorized that in the process of evolution, natural mutations had allowed certain species to survive changing conditions on earth while other would simply die out. This "survival of the fittest" concept was adopted by social Darwinists to justify both racism and the policies of imperialism.

Francis Galton

But it was the emergence of "scientific" eugenics in the late-nineteenth century that gave these ideas a veneer of credibility. In the final decades of the nineteenth century, Sir Francis Galton published a series of articles and books on heredity. His conclusion—that intelligence was inherited—stunned the world. His work seemed to justify the prevailing racist visions of the inferiority of certain racial and ethnic groups.

Cattell, Binet, and Simon

Galton's colleague, James Cattell from Columbia University, built on Galton's theories and developed a series of mental tests. Shortly thereafter, Alfred Binet was commissioned by the French Ministry of Public Instruction to develop a standardized test to identify "learning disabled children." Later, Binet's collaboration with his student Theodore Simon in 1905 led to the development of the famous Binet-Simon Scale, the first true "intelligence test."

Diagnosis versus Exclusion

But while the Binet-Simon Scale was designed as a diagnostic instrument to identify (and then help) children with learning problems, standardized tests soon took on a more sinister aspect. In 1912, Henry H. Goddard, often referred to as the "father of intelligence testing," used the Binet-Simon Scale as a way to classify individuals with low IQ scores as "morons, imbeciles and idiots."

These tests and their pernicious and hurtful labels, moreover, were used to classify immigrants arriving at Ellis Island and deport "undesirables." Later, Goddard would boast that because of his tests, "the numbers of aliens deported because of feeblemindedness . . . increased approximately 350 percent in 1913 and 570 percent in 1914." Clearly, standardized testing had become an instrument of exclusion and sorting rather than a diagnostic tool.

WORLD WAR I: A TURNING POINT

But the real breakthrough for the acceptance of mental testing came during World War I. As the war in Europe raged after 1914, Robert Yerkes, then president of the American Psychological Association (APA), began to lobby politicians and military leaders to begin using mental testing to "increase the efficiency of the Army and Navy."

When the United States entered the war in 1917, Yerkes created the APA's Psychological Examination of Recruits Committee to convince political leaders of the importance of mental testing in the military. While there was general skepticism, the military eventually agreed and gave Yerkes a commission as major in the "Sanitary Corps."

The Alpha Test

Yerkes immediately recruited more than 40 young psychologists to work on the project. They soon developed a battery of exams, commonly referred to as the Alpha tests, and tested more than 8,000 military recruits. This success led to more testing, and then, in 1918, General "Blackjack" Pershing issued his famous General Order 74 that gave full the support of the military to these new standardized tests. By the end of the war, more than 2 million recruits had been tested.

The Impact of the Alpha Test

There were two major impacts of the Alpha (and later Beta) tests during the war. The first was the "shock troops" of young psychologists recruited by Yerkes from private practice and universities throughout the country. These men would promote the use of standardized tests for the next generation. Their gravitas as part of the successful war effort would provide sustained support for these exams outside the military and into the corporations and schools of America.

Additionally, these standardized examinations had captured the imagination of the American people. The general feeling was that we finally had a scientific instrument that could accurately measure intelligence and help sort individuals. A new era had begun.

Standardized Tests and Schools

Even before the war ended, Yerkes had received hundreds of inquiries from school administrators throughout the country requesting a standardized test designed for schools. As a result of this enthusiastic groundswell of support for these exams, in 1919 the Education Board of the Rockefeller Foundation granted the National Research Council $25,000 to develop an exam for schools.

National Achievement Test

The result of this work led to the creation of the National Achievement Test, and by the early 1920s, more than 800,000 copies had been sent to schools. By 1923, it was estimated that more than 2,500,000 intelligence tests had been printed and were ready to be administered. The standardized test with its one-size-fits-all approach was no longer a novelty—it had become an article of faith among administrators and many educators.

Horace Mann Bond Responds

It was during this frenzied moment in educational history that a young Horace Mann Bond took a stand. Rather than blindly accepting these new "scientific instruments" as the future of educational assessment, he began to question the foundation of the exams themselves. His simple argument was that they were biased against African Americans, other people of color, and immigrants.

The catalyst for this criticism was a book published by Carl Brigham, one of Yerkes's "shock troops" that helped to develop and administer the Alpha and Beta tests during World War I. Brigham's work had a number of major conclusions that Bond rejected out of hand. But the most damning of them was that "of all the racial groups, negroes had the lowest intelligence."

"Intelligence Tests and Propaganda"

Bond's now classic article, "Intelligence Testing and Propaganda," was published in *The Crisis* with the enthusiastic support of W. E. B. Du Bois. In it, he argued that Brigham's racist claims were intended to justify both the reduced funding for black schools and the restrictive immigration legislation under the National Origins Acts.

With the publication of the article, this 19-year-old man stood firmly against public opinion as well as the lockstep policies of the educational community. He challenged both the scientific validity of standardized testing in schools and the growing acceptance of eugenics that was sweeping across the nation.

Bond summarized his position when he wrote that "it has ever been the bane of any development in science that its results in the hands [of] ... biased observers may be twisted to [become] weapons for the prejudiced." And indeed, the use of these flawed instruments had clearly been twisted.

The publication of *The Crisis* article in 1924 had not only challenged the juggernaut of standardized testing as an unbiased "scientific" measure of intelligence, but it also catapulted Horace Mann Bond into the forefront of the modern civil rights movement. The following month, Bond published another article in *Opportunity*, the official organ of the National Urban League.

"What the Army Intelligence Tests Measured"

In this searing critique of Brigham's racist vision of African American intelligence, Bond wrote that "all tests so far devised . . . and all so called racial differences identified can be resolved into social differences." Here Bond drew from the work of W. E. B. Du Bois in his classic study *The Philadelphia Negro*, by noting that differences between blacks and whites were due to environmental factors and not heredity.

Bond went on to write that Brigham had shown that test scores among blacks from northern states were higher than those of most whites from the south. This one finding, he argued, contradicted the racist, eugenics-based interpretation of the differences in test scores.

Nurture over Nature

Later Bond would publish another pathbreaking article in *The Crisis*, titled "Some Exceptional Negro Children," demonstrating that with the proper educational support, black children could do exceptionally well on standardized examinations. Bond showed that in his classroom of 30 black children from Chicago, almost two-thirds scored above 106 on the Stanford–Binet test, while more than a quarter scored over 130, a level achieved by only 1 percent of test takers, black or white.

The Environmentalist Interpretation

Bond went on to argue that the home environment of children was the key to their success. Exposure to reading material in the home, he wrote, matched with parental support and intellectual stimulation in the classroom accounted for most of the variation in the test scores of children.

This environmentalist interpretation was a powerful counterpoint to the hereditary argument that had become so popular during these years. Moreover, it challenged one of the accepted cornerstones of the eugenics movement.

Slow Reassessment of Standardized Tests

Although eugenics and its reliance on standardized testing would continue to dominate the thinking of many politicians and educators through the 1920s and 1930s, the intellectual challenge posed by Bond and others slowly undermined its efficacy. In 1930, for example, Brigham formally recanted much of his original racist argument in his "Intelligence Tests and Immigrant Groups," published in *Psychological Review*.

Eugenics and the Holocaust

And yet the struggle was far from over. The racist hereditarian arguments embedded in the theories of eugenics (and given false credibility by standardized tests) would become a powerful vehicle of anti-Semitism among Nazis in Hitler's Germany in the 1930s and during World War II. Our growing understanding of hereditarianism's direct connection to the Holocaust, however, appears to have undermined these vicious theories.

Nevertheless, recent history has demonstrated that they have not been completely eliminated from our world. By the late 1950s, for example, there was a resurgence of these eugenics-based interpretations of race and ethnicity as the civil rights movement began to gain steam in the United States. Critics of desegregation resurrected many of the eugenic/hereditarian arguments concerning the intellectual inferiority of African Americans.

While many of these arguments were repeated by southern politicians, they gained intellectual support as well. In 1958, Audrey Shuey published her incendiary book, *The Testing of Negro Intelligence*. Shuey argued that in her review of more than 300 studies of intelligence testing, "without a doubt" African Americans were intellectually inferior to whites. Later Shuey's dissertation advisor, Carleton Putnam, resurrected what has been called the "mulatto argument," which asserted that since George Washington Carver had blue eyes, his genius was due to his "white blood."

Horace Mann Bond had remained quiescent on the issue of bias in standardized exams since his early days at the University of Chicago. He had spent much of his career as a powerful educational administrator at several historically black colleges including Dillard University, Fisk University, and Fort Valley State University.

Bond's Collaboration Efforts

Nevertheless, he remained committed to the civil rights movement throughout his career. In 1953, for example, he collaborated with John Hope Franklin and C. Vann Woodward and provided important arguments against the *Plessy v. Ferguson* presumption of "separate but equal" facilities for public schools.

But when he read the works of Shuey, Putnam, and others, he was outraged. The result of this was his powerful book review, titled "Cat on a Hot Tin Roof," of Shuey's *The Testing of Negro Intelligence*. In this review, Bond restated many of the anti-eugenics arguments that he had made during the 1920s.

He then wrote that Shuey's work was little more than a poorly argued polemic. Bond noted that her book was simply another faulty argument against school desegregation, wrapped in a quasi-intellectual veneer. Bond wrote that Shuey was closely associated with the segregationist group, White Citizen's Council of the United States, and she had provided members of the group copies of her book free of charge.

Bond Attacks the "Southern Manifesto"

Later Bond wrote an interesting parody of white segregationists in the south entitled "Racially Stuffed Shirts and Other Enemies of Mankind." Here he made fun of the 1956 "Southern Manifesto," which promised unified political resistance to the U.S. Supreme Court's *Brown v. Board of Education* decision. Bond noted that the signatories of this racist policy document had all attended colleges in the lowest 10 percent of all institutions of higher learning in the United States.

While Bond later regretted the viciousness of his attack, he was successful in using both parody and intellectually constructed arguments throughout his career to challenge racist arguments as well as their underlying eugenics.

The formal and informal collaboration of W. E. B. Du Bois and Horace Mann Bond had an important impact on African American equity in education. Du Bois's demand for equal educational opportunities for blacks and whites, as well as his criticism of policies for "tracking" African American children into a vocational curriculum based primarily on skin color, gradually took hold in American education.

Similarly, Horace Mann Bond's criticism of the culturally biased nature of standardized examinations would gain traction during the course of the twentieth century. Although we have only recently recognized that standardized exams are not the ultimate scientific solution to understanding differences among students, it was this 19-year-old man who first stood against the rising tide of acceptance of these instruments and set the stage for a reassessment of their efficacy.

PROBLEMS REMAIN

And yet, when Bond first challenged standardized exams in the 1920s, enormous problems remained. Primary and secondary schools throughout the nation remained segregated either because of de facto residential patterns or de jure fiat. And for the most part, colleges, universities, medical schools, and law schools were essentially closed to African Americans.

It was in this restrictive environment that a new generation of civil rights activists took a stand. Once again, it was an informal collaboration between these young men and women and the well-established institutions of the NAACP and the NUL (National Urban League) that would address these fundamental problems.

As we have seen, the NAACP was established in the early twentieth century by African American activists led by Du Bois and others. Now, a new generation would take center stage in the movement and build on the NAACP's important work.

THE "NEW NEGROES"

This new generation of activists was led by individuals often referred to as the "new Negroes." Many of these new activists, born in the early twentieth century, were veterans of World War I. These men had enlisted in the U.S. Army and fought gallantly in segregated units in the trenches of France. Their idealistic notion was that because they had served their country, they would be granted equality and freedom when they returned from the war.

Sadly, the hopes of these brave men were shattered when they came home. The racial discrimination that they experienced when they left for Europe was alive and well when they returned to the United States.

CHARLES HAMILTON HOUSTON

One of the most influential of these "new Negro" activists was Charles Hamilton Houston. Like other African Americans of his generation, Houston enlisted in the army and served as an officer with distinction in France during World War I.

Before his tour of duty in France, Houston briefly served as judge advocate at Fort Meade, Maryland. Houston did not have his law degree, but had legal experience working in his father's law firm. In one of his cases, Houston dismissed charges against a black sergeant and as a result was severely reprimanded by the all-white judicial corps. Later he recalled this incident, writing that, "The hate and scorn showered on us Negro Officers by our fellow Americans convinced me that there was no sense in my dying for a world ruled by them."

World War I: A Turning Point

This event and the horrific experiences Houston endured as an infantry officer during the war had a dramatic impact on the young man. He wrote, "I made up my mind that if I ever got through this war, I would study law and use my time fighting for men who could not strike back."

Activism upon His Return

Despite the discrimination he endured upon his return, Houston enrolled at Harvard Law School. He then went on to become the first black student to be elected to the editorial board of the *Harvard Law Review*. Houston graduated *cum laude* with a JD in law in 1923.

Houston maintained his social activism throughout this period. In 1924, for example, after he was admitted to the bar, he became a founding member of the Washington Bar Association, an affiliate of the National Bar Association. This group was an alternative bar association that challenged the restrictive racial admission policies of the American Bar Association.

Then, in 1929, Houston was asked to serve as dean of Howard Law School, a position he held until 1935. During this critical period, he mentored hundreds of young black law students, many of whom would go on to have distinguished careers and become important social activists for racial equality.

Houston Mentors Thurgood Marshall

Certainly, the most important of his many protégés was Thurgood Marshall. Although Marshall was not his best student, Houston recognized that young Thurgood had strong desire to change the world and improve the lives of African Americans. Together, they would do just that.

Under Houston's mentorship, Marshall became a fine student and graduated from Howard in 1933, first in his class. Marshall then joined the NAACP and became part of Houston's legal team. The goal of the team was to challenge the segregationist policies that had blocked African Americans from attending law schools throughout the nation.

Murray v. Pearson

Marshall was assigned an important case involving Donald Gaines Murray, who had been denied admission to the University of Maryland School of Law because of its segregationist policies. Marshall employed an unusual strategy, first developed by Nathan Marigold, by using the infamous *Plessy v. Ferguson* decision to his advantage.

Marshall argued that by denying Murray admission, the University of Maryland Law School had directly violated the *Plessy* decision. The Maryland Court of Appeals ruled in favor of Marshall (*Murray v. Pearson*) noting that "compliance with the Constitution cannot be deferred at the will of the state."

While the doors of law schools throughout the nation did not swing open widely because of this decision, there clearly was a crack in their segregationist policies. In the following decades, dozens of law schools reluctantly admitted African American students, and a core group of young black activists made their way into the courtrooms of America.

Marshall and the LDF

The *Murray v. Pearson* decision also had a profound impact on Marshall himself. First, because of his innovative approach to the case, he gained instant recognition and *gravitas* not only among black activists, but in the wider legal community as well. And perhaps more importantly, because of his success in the *Murray* case, he helped establish the NAACP's Legal Defense and Educational Fund (LDF) in 1940 and became its first executive director.

Marshall recruited hundreds of young black lawyers to his team throughout the years and, through his leadership, guided the LDF to a new level of judicial success. The LDF fought to dismantle Jim Crow laws and seek equality in American education. In addition to winning a number of cases in the lower courts, the LDF under the leadership of Marshall and Houston guided a number of important cases all the way to the U.S. Supreme Court.

Voting Rights and Race Covenants

In 1944, for example, the LDF successfully shepherded the *Smith v. Allwright* voting rights case to the U.S. Supreme Court. This early voting rights case challenged a Texas law that prohibited African Americans from voting in primary elections. Then, in 1948, racial housing covenants were struck down with in *Shelley v. Kraemer*.

Despite the death of Charles Hamilton Houston in April 1950, the LDF, under Marshall's direction, continued to struggle for equality in educational facilities and equal access to schools. In June 1950, for example, Marshall successfully argued the *McLaurin v. Oklahoma State Regents for Higher Education* before the U.S. Supreme Court.

In this case, George McLaurin, an African American, was denied admission to the doctoral program in education at Oklahoma State University solely because of his race. Here the court ruled unanimously that this decision was a violation of the equal protection clause of the Fourteenth Amendment to the U.S. Constitution.

The decisive victories in these and other U.S. Supreme Court cases empowered and encouraged the LDF of the NAACP, and the legal defense attorneys under Marshall. It also prepared Marshall and his team for the biggest and most important civil rights challenge associated with education, *Brown v. Board of Education of Topeka*.

BROWN V. BOARD OF EDUCATION

On its surface, the *Brown v. Board of Education* case was relatively simple, but its impact on American society was dramatic. Moreover, it helped to launch the contemporary civil rights movement. The case involved young Linda Brown, who wanted to attend an all-white school that was relatively close to her home. But because of racial segregation laws in Kansas, she was denied admittance. Rather, she had a long walk and a longer bus ride each day to attend the all-black public school for Negroes.

Linda's father, Reverend Brown, with the support of the local black community, sought relief from the court, but the case was denied because of the "separate but equal doctrine" of the *Plessy v. Ferguson* decision of 1896. It was at this point in December 1952 that the LDF under Marshall took up the *Brown* case and began litigation.

A NEW TACTIC

While Marshall had built his reputation as an attorney in the *Murray* case by turning the *Plessy v. Ferguson* decision on its head and using its racist premise to secure equal rights for African Americans, he changed directions for the *Brown* case. Marshall gambled that a more appropriate tactic was to use the equal protection clause of the Fourteenth Amendment of the Constitution as the basis of his argument, just as he had in the 1950 *McLaurin* case.

SUCCESS IN *BROWN*

After much deliberation, the justices of the Supreme Court, led by Chief Justice Warren, eventually ruled unanimously in favor of Linda Brown and struck down the infamous *Plessy v. Ferguson* decision. This law, they ruled, was indeed a violation of the Fourteenth amendment to the Constitution, as Marshall had argued.

While the *Brown v. Board of Education* decision in 1954 and its companion decision in 1955 did not end racial injustice, it opened the door to a new perspective and a new attitude regarding equality and was a catalyst for the modern civil rights movement. It's no exaggeration to argue that the energy of today's "Black Lives Matter" movement has its roots in the flood of positive social change triggered by the work of Marshall and those who came before him.

THE BROAD ARC OF EDUCATIONAL CHANGE

The broad arc of twentieth-century racial activism began with W. E. B. Du Bois's demand to end racial tracking in education and offer African American children the same opportunities afforded whites. Moreover, his work on educational equality was a cornerstone in the creation of the NAACP. This organization sought social justice and equality through the courts and represented a direct collaborative link between Du Bois and other activists of this period.

COLLABORATION

Du Bois's work as the long-time editor of *The Crisis*, the official organ of the NAACP, nurtured hundreds of young black scholars who carried on these activities. Among them was Horace Mann Bond, who single-handedly stood against the tide of standardized exams sweeping the nation beginning in the 1920s. By recognizing the inherent racial bias in these instruments, Bond challenged both racism and its dangerous first cousin, eugenics.

The final collaborative link between the early work of Du Bois and the modern-day civil rights movement can be seen in the work of Charles Hamilton Houston and future Supreme Court Justice, Thurgood Marshall. It was through the NAACP that these two men centered their activism, first by challenging Jim Crow segregation laws that restricted African Americans from attending law schools in many states.

Their success in these critical legal actions led to a flood of idealistic black attorneys actively working for racial justice and equality throughout the twentieth century. In addition, their success led to the creation of the NAACP's legal defense fund (LDF) that has become an engine of racial equality since its creation in 1940 and provided legal leverage in the struggle for achieving the *Brown v. Board of Education* decision.

As Dr. Martin Luther King noted in his famous speech given at the National Cathedral on March 31, 1968, "The arc of the moral universe is long, but it bends towards justice."

Chapter 10

The Arc of Educational Change

The arc of educational change has a long and dramatic history. From the early writings of the foundationalists beginning in the late 1500s to the present day, the struggle for educational change has been the result of a profound collaborative effort among philosophers, educators, and everyday people.

THE EFFECT OF COLLABORATION

In American classrooms, change also has been triggered by persistent collaboration. Among these was the determined efforts of educators to promote a more child-centered learning environment, and make a dramatic shift toward secular education as well as more compassionate discipline of young children.

The net effect of this collaboration has led to broad societal changes. These include the slow but consistent progress toward social justice and equality for women, African Americans, immigrants, and working people. In addition, these collaborative efforts have yielded greater opportunities for the American people and a slow but growing acceptance of diversity in our nation.

BARRIERS TO CHANGE

And yet there have been persistent barriers to educational change. Perhaps the most important of these is the authoritarian, top-down, subject-centered approach to teaching. The persistence of this traditional method may be the result of the "comfort of the familiar"—the reliance on "tried and true" habits of classroom teaching and school administration. The difficulty that John Dewey had in sustaining his progressive Lab School classroom methods is but one example of how educational change can be subverted.

PARENTAL REJECTION OF CHANGE

Parental rejection of educational change has also been a persistent problem. Whether it was nineteenth-century parents who demanded stricter discipline and corporal punishment in the classroom or the contemporary parental rights movement that has challenged the role of teachers and their selection of reading material and curriculum, some parents have always been a consistent barrier to positive educational change.

CONSERVATIVE PARSIMONY

And then there is conservative parsimony. This has been a consistent barrier to educational development. The reluctance of the public to financially support education has a long history. The monumental work of Horace Mann in the mid-nineteenth century to convince the American people of the need for public support of education illustrates this problem. And today, the declining support for public education as well as even modest increases in teacher salaries by state legislatures demonstrates the persistence of this problem.

THE BUSINESS MODEL

Related to the ongoing parsimony by state and local governments has been the emergence of school consolidation beginning in the early twentieth century, along with standardization of the curriculum and testing of both students and teachers. These measures follow the distinctive pattern established by the business community to ensure profitability and maintain productivity.

The adoption of the "business model" for education has been disastrous. While business is a private good, education is not. As a public good, education is focused on individual learning and does not operate to either promote productivity or profit.

CONTEMPORARY EDUCATIONAL MALAISE

This brings us to the educational malaise that we are experiencing today. The distinctive anti-democratic movement of the last few decades has yielded a virulent populism and spawned a resurgence of patriarchy, homophobia, and white nationalism. These vicious patterns have played out in the classrooms of the nation and have had a significant impact on the process of positive educational change.

HOPE FOR THE FUTURE

And yet, despite these major barriers, both in the past and in our contemporary world, positive educational change persists. The arc of educational change is unrelenting and, as we have seen, the collaborative spirit has overcome these barriers in the past and will in the future.

THE FOUNDATIONALISTS

Our story of the success of collaboration and networking in educational history begins with the great work of the foundationalists. As we have noted, this group of scholars and activists represented a decentralized form of intellectual collaboration. While some of these figures including Francis Bacon, John Locke, Voltaire, and Jean-Jacques Rousseau engaged directly, their collaborative efforts also were based on the careful reading of each other's works and critically expanding these ideas with their own.

PRE-ENLIGHTENMENT SCHOLARS

The first of the foundationalists figures introduced here was Francis Bacon (1561–1626), one of the leading lights of empiricism. Bacon argued that critical observation and inductive reasoning was at the heart of science. Though not a contemporary of Bacon, John Locke (1632–1700) was profoundly influenced by Bacon's rejection of the concept of "innate knowledge" derived from Christianity.

This form of "deductive philosophy" was seen as contrary to both empirical observation and inductive reasoning, and therefore wholly out of step with the emergence of scientific analysis. For Locke, all knowledge was derived from experiences and education.

ENLIGHTENMENT SCHOLARS

Voltaire (1694–1778), the great French Enlightenment figure, was less a philosopher than either Bacon or Locke, but his rejection of religion and his demand for a clear separation of church and state opened the door to the secular foundation of modern education.

Voltaire's contemporary, Jean-Jacques Rousseau (1712–1778), expanded these and other ideas of the great foundationalists and argued not only for secular education but, like Locke, rejected corporal punishment of children. In addition, Rousseau argued that "man was born free but is everywhere in chains." This new vision of the humanity and the innate intelligence of children brought a new child-centered perspective to education.

Johann Heinrich Pestalozzi (1746–1827) applied many of these intellectual ideas in the classroom. Through his innovative educational novels he introduced the world to child-centered learning. His influence was broad; Froebel and Montessori were profoundly influenced by his work, and even Albert Einstein was impressed with his child-centered approach.

As a young boy, Einstein attended a Pestalozzian schools in Aarau, Switzerland, and later wrote that "it made me clearly realize how much superior an education based on free action and personal responsibility is to one relying on outward authority."

ADVOCATES FOR THE POOR

By the late eighteenth and early nineteenth centuries, a handful of advocates of the poor moved from philosophy to activism. Here, the decentralized form of movement collaboration created a profound shift in education that embraced a form of universal education designed not only for the very rich, but also the poor. These collaborative efforts began with eighteenth-century Quaker activists such as George Fox, Thomas Budd, and John Woodman, who provided a model of education for society's most oppressed group of men and women—enslaved and free blacks.

JOSEPH LANCASTER

Quaker advocacy for both the abolition of slavery and the education of African Americans met with a great deal of resistance, but also inspired a new generation of activists who sought to improve the condition of these oppressed men and women. Among these was Joseph Lancaster who, as a young boy, was profoundly moved by the plight of the enslaved and who later advocated for the "new poor" in England, the United States, and a number of countries in central and south America.

As part of Lancaster's efforts to educate the poor, he developed pedagogical techniques that have had a lasting influence on modern methods of teaching. Among these was the "monitorial system" in which more advanced students taught younger ones in small groups. Today this form peer teaching has been shown to have a positive impact on some students. Lancaster also rewarded student excellence with prizes (stars and stickers today) and developed a unique graded approach to education.

The collaborative reform efforts of Quaker activists and educational entrepreneurs such as Joseph Lancaster opened the door to the idea of universal education and provided new approaches to teaching.

EDUCATION FOR DEMOCRACY

As the revolutionary ideas of the Enlightenment spread throughout Europe and in the colonies in the eighteenth century, the Founding Fathers in the American colonies began to link their new democratic experiment with fresh perspectives on education. For statesmen such as Thomas Jefferson, Benjamin Franklin, and Benjamin Rush, the success of this new experiment in democracy could only be secured with the support of an educated nation.

While each of these important figures had a different vision for the new nation, their intellectual collaboration contributed to our growing appreciation of the importance of education.

Thomas Jefferson

Jefferson is often praised for promoting higher education in the United States, especially through his efforts to establish the University of Virginia in 1819. But he was also active in supporting both primary and secondary education. Jefferson introduced his important Bill 79 to the Virginia Legislature in 1778, and it was eventually passed into law in 1796 as an "Act to Establish Public Schools." This bill opened the door to universal education in the United States.

Benjamin Franklin

Jefferson's close friend and colleague, Benjamin Franklin, also was an advocate for education in both the colonies and later in the new United States. Franklin's work was broad and focused on academies, professional schools, colleges for women, as well adult and African American education.

Franklin established the Philadelphia Academy in 1749. This was a monumental achievement for secondary education in the colonies. Later, in 1791, the academy would expand and eventually become the University of Pennsylvania. This premier institution graduated hundreds of statesmen, lawyers, and scholars with 21 of these serving as members of the Continental Congress, 9 as signees of the Declaration of Independence, and 5 who signed the U.S. Constitution.

Benjamin Rush

Finally, Benjamin Rush, an associate of both Jefferson and Franklin, had a different focus on education, arguing that religion should be an important part of the curriculum. But like his deist friend Jefferson and agnostic colleague Franklin, he saw universal education as essential for the survival of our democratic republic.

Rush perceived education as a vehicle to create what he called "republican machines," citizens who would appreciate the basic ideals and value of democracy. As such, he favored teacher training and the establishment of colleges in every state as well as a national university to train exceptional students in politics and international affairs.

The intellectual collaboration of these three founding fathers provided a framework for the future of education in the United States. Their emphasis on the central importance of education to preserve our fragile democratic experiment; their advocacy of an educational ladder from the primary grades, secondary schools, and academies through universities; and their promotion of universal education for the poor, women, and African Americans was a remarkable educational blueprint for the nation.

THE TENTH AMENDMENT

But the grand and idealistic educational ideas of these and other Founding Fathers were crushed with the ratification of the infamous Tenth Amendment in 1791. This amendment essentially deferred to the states all the powers that were not directly mentioned in the Constitution itself. While the Tenth Amendment was seen as an important compromise to secure the support of some representatives, it had a devastating impact on education in the United States, especially for women, minorities, and the poor.

Unlike the idealistic plans of the Founding Fathers, political leaders in individual states were more parochial and not especially concerned with providing funds for education. Typically, they preferred that churches, tutors, and private schools attend to this important function as they had in the past. Sadly, it would be more than a half-century before states slowly began to recognize their important responsibility to support education for their citizens.

EMMA WILLARD

It was this difficult environment that Emma Willard found herself. When she established her legendary Troy Female Seminary in 1821, it had been almost a half-century since the signing of the Declaration of Independence and decades since the idea of female education had been seen as important to the nation through the concept of "Republican Motherhood."

Because of their lack of access to education at most levels, including primary education in some communities, women traditionally had been seen as intellectually inferior to men and not worth the investment. The common argument against female education during this period was that by allocating funds to educate women, fewer dollars would be available to teach men.

Emma Willard challenged this parsimonious vision and rejected the intellectually inferior "finishing schools" that were popular for the daughters of wealthy planters, merchants, and proprietors. Emma argued that women should have access to schools with a rigorous curriculum that was comparable to those of men.

But because there was little support for such a school, she took matters into her own hands. With the generous support of a number of benefactors, she established her Troy Female Seminary that embraced both a rigorous academic curriculum as well as teacher training.

Although a tireless advocate for female education and teacher training, Emma was not alone. Her collaboration with colleagues and her students created an educational tsunami that would spread the ideas of female education throughout the nation.

Emma Willard's Collaborative Network

One of her students, Elizabeth Cady Stanton, for example, was a central figure in the early women's movement and instrumental in the Seneca Falls Convention in 1848. Perhaps less well known were teachers who were trained at the Troy Seminary, such as Julia Pierpoint, who helped Emma establish her seminary and then went on to become the headmistress of the South Carolina Female Collegiate Institute.

Julia modeled her curriculum after that of the Troy Female Seminary and during the course of 12 years graduated more than 4,000 young women, many of whom became teachers and who would spread the idea of the importance of female education. One such graduate was Anna Maria Calhoun Clemson who, with her husband, founded Clemson University.

The Legacy of Troy Female Seminary

Emma's struggle for female education had a ripple effect on the nation. Women eventually came to be seen as the most effective teachers for younger children and soon dominated education in the primary grades. In addition, women were gradually seen as intellectually equal to men, attending and excelling in secondary schools and universities. The movement collaboration of Emma Willard, her family, her colleagues, and her students had a profound and lasting effect on American education.

THE COMMON SCHOOL

While advocates for both the poor and gender equity would continue through the nineteenth century, the nation still lacked a systematic educational system. However, as the economy was transformed by the market revolution and Industrial Revolution, Americans slowly began to understand the importance of education for their children. Local communities as well as states eventually responded. By the mid-nineteenth century, education was no longer simply a "nice thing" but was central to our national security, our democracy, and our economy.

Farmers, Workers, and Businessmen

Commercial farmers, workingmen organizations, small business owners, as well as hundreds of political activists began to demand that states take this responsibility seriously. It is not surprising that leadership in this effort came from Massachusetts, the birthplace of "public" schools during the seventeenth century. These Puritan schools were unique in the American colonies and while they were far from universal, they did place Massachusetts at the forefront of education during this period.

Whig Party

The coordinated pressure of pro-education groups combined with the reform orientation of the Massachusetts state Whig Party eventually overcame the parsimony and reluctance of some legislators to create a State Board of Education headed by Horace Mann. While the board was given little power, Mann used his "bully pulpit" to convince both his colleagues in the legislature and the people of Massachusetts to establish what was called the common school.

This form of public/private collaboration was a success. In addition, Horace Mann's leadership and activism was critical. The philosophical and rational arguments he made in his *Common School Journal* not only convinced his colleagues and the people of Massachusetts, but also alerted leaders in other states of the importance of not only universal education but also a common set of cultural and patriotic values that would bind the nation together.

In the years that followed, Henry Bernard, Calvin Wiley, and David Perkins Page along with an army of idealistic young teachers would transform the nation.

A CURRICULUM FOR THE NATION

But while the common schools were taking root in a number of northern and western states during this period, students typically lacked the basic supplies necessary to learn. The most glaring of these was the lack of books, much less a set of readers that would support the common school experiment.

Many students used family Bibles or books borrowed from their friends and relatives for reading instruction. For their lessons in subjects such as arithmetic and geography, teachers had to be creative and design and write instructional materials themselves. In larger communities, students might use worn-out copies of *The New England Primer* or another version of that ancient reader for lessons. But clearly, the nation needed a unified set of learning materials that would ensure the success of the common school.

William McGuffey

It was into this educational vacuum that a humble Presbyterian minister and teacher by the name of William McGuffey made his important contribution with his *McGuffey Reader* series. But he was not alone in this effort. As a young professor at Miami University in Ohio, McGuffey traveled throughout the state, advocating for common schools to be established. Soon he met Lyman Beecher, who had recently moved to Cincinnati, and joined with a group of reformers in what we call the Cincinnati Circle.

Cincinnati Circle

The Cincinnati Circle was composed of some of the leading educational reformers of the day. These included Catherine Beecher and her sister, Harriet Beecher Stowe, who were advocates of abolition, common schools, and women's education. Lyman Beecher, the patriarch of the Beecher family and reform advocate, was the informal leader of the group. Other luminaries such as Edward Mansfield, the first superintendent of Ohio's common schools and Joseph Ray, author of the famous *Ray's Arithmetic* series, also were in the group.

In fact, it was Harriet Beecher who recommended McGuffey to publishers Truman & Smith of Cincinnati to write and edit a new series of *Readers* for students in the common schools. McGuffey accepted the offer and created a set of *Readers* that provided the nation with new books promoting a graded approach to reading, as well as a common set of patriotic and moral values. In addition, through his collaboration with members of the Cincinnati Circle, McGuffey set a new pedagogical direction in teaching.

These *Readers* rejected the age-old methods of memorization and recitation and suggested a new child-centered approach to education. Clearly this collaborative association changed the way that teachers taught, and children learned. The new common school movement now had its basic educational tools. Things would never be the same for American education.

SOME SUCCESS

The collaborative efforts of early Quaker activists, combined with the work of idealistic educators such as Joseph Lancaster and his army of monitors, alerted the world to the importance of educating the most vulnerable members of society. Similarly, gender equity advocates such as Emma Willard, her colleagues, and her students brought women into the classrooms of the nation both as students and then gradually as teachers in American schools.

Then, the ongoing collaboration of grassroots groups such as workingmen organizations, new commercial farmers, progressive political leaders, and educational reformers such as Horace Mann, Henry Bernard, and Calvin Wiley brought the common school movement to the attention of the American people. With the collaborative curriculum reform efforts of the Cincinnati Circle that included the Beecher family, William McGuffey, Joseph Ray, and others, the common school now had books and lessons that would support education for the next half-century and beyond.

"ORIGINAL SIN" OF AMERICA

But despite these accomplishments, by the mid-nineteenth century the "original sin" of American society continued to plague the nation. This "sin" was the institution of slavery and the disregard for the humanity of African Americans. While millions of white children of all ages were attending common schools by the 1850s, in many states of the growing union, young enslaved children were left further and further behind.

To be clear, while the abolitionist movement of mid-nineteenth century was gaining strength and the clarion call for social and political reform was becoming stronger, it would take a civil war to end this disgraceful institution. That war would devastate the nation with more than 600,000 servicemen killed during its bloody onslaught.

FREEDMEN'S BUREAU SCHOOLS

When the carnage ended, and the nation entered a period known as Reconstruction in 1865, a public/private collaborative partnership developed with the creation of the Freedmen's Bureau and especially the Bureau's schools. The Freedmen's Bureau schools brought together activists within the religious community, political reformers from the new progressive Republican party, as well as an army of idealistic teachers—black, white, women and men—in one of the most challenging educational experiments ever conceived.

The Freedmen's Bureau schools were a great success, though short-lived in the toxic environment of the Reconstruction South. All told, more than 9,000 teachers were engaged to teach African American children and adults. About 4,000 schools were established, and it has been estimated that more than 200,000 students were exposed to the rudiments of education during its brief existence.

The collaborative efforts of the Freedmen's Bureau schools were remarkable. Its success demonstrated that the public and private sectors of the economy could effectively work together, with the cooperation of idealistic reformers playing a central role. Throughout the years other forms of public/private collaboration, for example, the Civilian Conservation Corps, Vista, and the Peace Corps, have used this model.

Clearly, it was the Freedmen's Bureau schools that pushed the limits of this collaborative enterprise and brought African Americans one small step in the direction of educational equity. This was crucial in the overall civil rights and educational equity struggle that would follow in the next century.

PROGRESSIVE EDUCATION

By the end of the nineteenth century, American education had changed dramatically. The common schools and the graded schools in many cities were now accepted educational institutions. Moreover, the high school had made significant progress since mid-century. Combined with our growing college and university system, America had what appeared to be a strong educational ladder that would propel the nation into the next century.

And yet, many educational reformers were seriously concerned that our educational system was not up to the challenges of the day. Students were still reading McGuffey's *Readers* and Ray's classic arithmetic books, and while these venerated volumes may have been appropriate for an earlier generation of students, many feared that they simply did not reflect the needs of our growing industrial and technological economy.

PROGRESSIVE EDUCATION COLLABORATORS

As a result, a new generation of educational reformers collaborated to create innovative approaches to education that would guide the nation to the future. Francis Parker's famous Quincy Method, for example, centered on student experience over memorization and rote learning; William Kilpatrick's "project method" promoted "socially purposeful" acts to improve the community; while Maria Montessori's student-centered learning and John Dewey's concept of learning by doing were all elements of the new progressive education of this period.

While each of these progressive educators and dozens of others sought to improve education, most understood that the growing individualism of the late-nineteenth century had deprived students with the understanding of the importance of community and social responsibility.

Once again, the intellectual collaborative efforts of scholars and activists within the educational community would change the way we conceived of education—not simply as an accumulation of knowledge, but also as vehicle to regenerate American society from the classroom up.

AN INTELLECTUAL BRIDGE

The progressives also were an important intellectual bridge between foundationalists such as Johann Pestalozzi, Jean-Jacques Rousseau, and John Locke on the one hand, and the neo progressives and critical pedagogists of the present day. Their work collectively has transformed the world of education.

RACIAL EQUITY IN EDUCATION

But despite the important advances in education by the end of the nineteenth century, including the impressive work of the Freedman's Bureau schools following the American Civil War, African Americans continued to struggle to reach some form of racial equity in education.

External support from a number of well-meaning philanthropic and religious groups had helped, but true advancement in African American education often was the product of the collaborative efforts of black people themselves. This was especially important as the noxious effects of white supremacy energized Jim Crow. Moreover, the U.S. Supreme Court essentially gave federal support to segregation with its infamous *Plessy v. Ferguson* decision in 1896.

COLLABORATION FOR RACIAL EQUALITY

The intellectual and direct collaboration of some of the major figures in the civil rights movement galvanized the effort toward educational equity for African Americans. Among the most influential activists were W. E. B. Du Bois, Charles Hamilton Houston, Booker T. Washington, Horace Mann Bond, and Thurgood Marshall. While other men and women were important, the collaboration of these individuals was essential in the fight for educational equality.

W. E. B. Du Bois

Among these important figures, Du Bois stands out. As the first African American PhD from Harvard University in the field of history, Du Bois was a fierce advocate for equal opportunities for black students. He clashed with Booker T. Washington over the latter's vocational tracking approach to black education. Du Bois also was instrumental in establishing the NAACP and was the first editor of *The Crisis*, the association's journal that promoted civil rights and educational equity.

Horace Mann Bond

As editor, Du Bois took a young Horace Mann Bond under his wing and published Bond's article challenging standardized testing and its underlying contention that African Americans (and immigrants) were intellectually inferior. Bond would continue his criticism of these tests throughout his career, rejecting the racist hereditary arguments inherent in the eugenics movement.

Charles Hamilton Houston

Charles Hamilton Houston was another critical link in the educational equity chain. Houston, a distinguished veteran of World War I, was instrumental in mobilizing the power of the NAACP into an activist legal organization that challenged segregation at its roots. When Houston returned from France following the war, he entered Harvard Law school and eventually became a distinguished attorney, dean of Howard Law School, and the first general consul of the NAACP.

Houston's idea was to legally challenge segregation and promote educational equity by opening American law schools to African Americans. Black law school graduates would then pursue the cause of civil rights. This strategy was ultimately successful for two reasons. First, it produced an army of idealistic black lawyers who would confront segregation through peaceful legal means. And second, Houston was able to recruit Thurgood Marshall into the NAACP.

Thurgood Marshall

Together, Houston and Marshall would establish the Legal Defense Fund of the NAACP in 1940. This organization would struggle mightily to end racial segregation in American public schools. One of its crowning achievements was the famous *Brown v. Board of Education* decision that would mark the beginning of the end of legal racial segregation in schools.

Marshall would go on to a brilliant legal career and was eventually confirmed as an Associate Justice of the Supreme Court, the first African American to hold that position. The collaboration of these individuals was an inspiration to educators throughout the nation and, arguably, the world. Their intellectual and activist efforts would change the face of education and move it in a new progressive direction.

CRITICAL PEDAGOGY

The work of progressive activists and civil rights workers during the twentieth century had a dramatic effect on education. Americans were alerted to the importance of inclusion and diversity in schools and, by the last half of the twentieth century, real social change seemed possible.

And yet, educational scholars recognized that despite the changing attitudes of Americans, the curriculum of schools at the primary, secondary, and college level was far from progressive. Progressives lamented that the "great (white) men" of the past dominated our historical narrative and women, workers, African Americans, and immigrants were missing from our histories.

By the late 1960s, a group of "new social historians" including such figures as Paulo Freire began to question the conservative elements of history, sociology, and literature and focused their attention on "the oppressed" in our society. Other historians such as Howard Zinn centered their attention on women's history, labor history, and the history of immigration. These scholars and a host of others focused on individuals of the past who had been largely ignored, and helped to reshape the historical narrative.

In the field of education, a handful of activists challenged the conservative pedagogy of primary and secondary education. Ira Shor and his colleague Paulo Freire, for example, published *A Pedagogy for Liberation* in 1987, which encouraged both teachers and students to become activists in the learning process.

Others, such as Henry Giroux and Michael Apple, have continued this tradition. Giroux has called for a critical pedagogy that would help students become cultural and political activists to create a sustainable democracy. Michael Apple, on the other hand, has built on the ideas of the new social historians and has argued that the education curriculum has systematically excluded certain groups. He notes that by exposing the "hidden curriculum," schools would become more open and diversified and students would be able to think more critically about their world.

ONGOING CHALLENGES

This collective collaboration of new social historians and "critical pedagogists" has had an important impact on education. But like other progressive educational efforts in the past, their work has been challenged by a growing chorus of conservative historians, educators, and politicians. The bitter controversy over the publication of *The 1619 Project*, by *New York Times* journalist Nikole Hannah-Jones, demonstrates some of the obstacles to educational change. This is, of course, is as it has always been.

In many ways, the emergence of critical pedagogy in the second half of the twentieth century is the culmination of years of struggle for educational equity and diversity in the United States. Recently, racial equity advocates and critical pedagogists have sought to transform the curriculum of the nation, to diversify and transform our classrooms, and to create an educational system that is an engine of positive social change.

And yet, while the barriers to progress continue to challenge the inevitable arc of educational change, we may once again be reassured by the words of the great Reverend Martin Luther King Jr., who said, "The arc of the moral universe is long, but it bends toward justice."

From the work of the foundationalists to progressive educators, racial and gender equity advocates, neoprogressives, critical pedagogues, and thousands of collaborators, the arc of educational change is slowly bending toward inclusion, equity, and justice.

References

Appiah, K. A. (2014). *Lines of Descent: W. E. B. Du Bois and the Emergence of Identity*. Cambridge, MA: Harvard University Press.
Apple, M. (1979). *Ideology and Curriculum*, 4th ed. New York: Routledge.
Bacon, F. (2021). *The Proficience and Advancement of Learning*. San Francisco, CA: Blurb Publishing. Originally published in 1605.
Bacon, F. (2017). *Novum Organum*. Scotts Valley, CA: CreateSpace Independent Publishing. Originally published in 1620.
Bacon, F. (2018). *New Atlantis*. Mineola, NY: Dover Publications. Originally published in 1626.
Ball, H. (1998). *A Defiant Life: Thurgood Marshall and the Persistence of Racism in America*. New York: Crown Publications.
Baym, N. (1991). "Women and the Republic: Emma Willard's Rhetoric of History." *American Quarterly* 4:1, 1–23.
Baynton, D. (2016). *Defectives in the Land: Disability and Immigration in the Age of Eugenics*. Chicago: University of Chicago Press.
Best, J. H. (1962). *Benjamin Franklin on Education*. New York: Teachers College Press.
Blinderman, A. (1976). *Three Early Champions of Education: Benjamin Franklin, Benjamin Rush, and Noah Webster*. Bloomington, IN: Phi Delta Kappan.
Bond, H. M. (1924). "Intelligence Testing and Propaganda." *The Crisis Reader*, n.p.
Bond, H. M. (1924, July). "What the Army Intelligence Tests Measured." *Opportunity*, n.p.
Bond, H. M. (1925, June). "Temperament." *The Crisis Reader*, n.p.
Bond, H. M. (1958). "Cat on a Hot Tin Roof." *Journal of Negro Education* 27:4, 519–525.
Brigham, C. (2017). *A Study of American Intelligence*. New York: Andesite Press. Originally published in 1923.
Burton, W. (1852). *The District School as It Was*. Boston: P. R. Marvin.
Calhoun, D. (1984). "Eyes for the Jacksonian World: William C. Woodbridge and Emma Willard." *Journal of the Early Republic* 4: 1–26.
Campbell, J. (1967). *Colonel Francis W. Parker: The Children's Crusader*. New York: Teachers College Press.

Caton, J. (2018). *Biographical Sketch of John Dean Caton*. Edited by Robert Fergus. London: Forgotten Books. Originally published in 1882.
Clark, H. C., ed. (2016). *Encyclopedic Liberty: Political Articles in the Dictionary of Diderot and D'Alembert*. Indianapolis, IN: Liberty Fund.
Cremin, L. (1982). *American Education: The National Experience*. New York: Harper and Row.
Cubberley, E. P. (1919). *Public Education in the United States*. Boston: Houghton Mifflin Co.
Curti, M. (1935). *The Social Ideas of American Educators*. New York: Charles Scribner's Sons.
Damrosh, L. (2007). *Rousseau: Restless Genius*. Boston: Mariner Books.
Dewey, J. (2019). *Psychology*. New York: Wentworth Press. Originally printed in 1886.
Dewey, J. (1889). *Psychology: Introduction to the Principles and Practice of Education. The Early Works of John Dewey, Volume 1 (1882–1898)*. Carbondale: Southern Illinois University Press.
Dewey, J. (2008). *The Child and the Curriculum*. New York: Cosimo Classics. Originally published in 1902.
Dewey, J. (1916). *Democracy and Education: An Introduction to the Philosophy of Education*. New York: Macmillan.
Dewey, J. (2000). *Experience in Nature*. Mineola, NY: Dover Publications. Originally published in 1925.
Dewey, J. (1974). *Impressions of Soviet Russia and the Revolutionary World*. New York: Teachers College Press. Originally published in 1929.
Dewey, J. (1997). *Experience and Education*. New York: Free Press. Originally published in 1938.
Dewey, J. (1989). *Freedom and Culture*. Amherst, NY: Prometheus. Originally published in 1939.
Dewey, J., and E. Dewey. (1915). *Schools of To-Morrow*. New York: E. P. Dutton & Co.
Dickens, C. (1854). *Hard Times*. London: Bradbury and Evans.
Du Bois, W. E. B. (2014). *The Philadelphia Negro*. Oxford: Oxford University Press. Originally published in 1897.
Du Bois, W. E. B. (2016). *The Souls of Black Folk*. Mineola, NY: Dover Publications. Originally published in 1903.
Emerson, R. W. (2022). *Emerson's Essays: The Complete First and Second Series*. Columbia, SC: Independently published. Originally published in 1841; reprinted in 1844.
Finkelstein, B. (1989). *Governing the Young: Teacher Behavior in Popular Primary Schools in Nineteenth-Century United States*. New York: Falmer Press.
Freire, P. (1970). *Pedagogy of the Oppressed*. Trans. Myra Ramus. London: Bloomsbury Academic.
Friend, M., and L. Cooke. (2012). *Interactions: Collaborative Skills for School Professionals*. Hoboken, NJ: Prentice Hall.

Gibson, L. (2012). *Young Thurgood: The Making of a Supreme Court Justice*. Amhurst, NY: Prometheus Books.
Giroux, H. (2020). *On Critical Pedagogy*, 2nd ed. London: Bloomsbury Academic.
Guicciardini, F. (2019). *The History of Italy*. London: Wentworth Press. Originally published in 1561.
Hannah-Jones, N. (2021). *The 1619 Project*. New York: New York Times Co.
Harris, S., ed. (2003). *Women's Early Historical Narratives*. London: Penguin.
Hewitt, E. (1884). *A Treatise on Pedagogy for Young Teachers*. Cincinnati: Van Antwerp, Bragg & Company.
Hogan, D. (1989). "The Market Revolution and Disciplinary Power: Joseph Lancaster and the Psychology of the Early Classroom System." *History of Education Quarterly* 29:3, 381–417.
Horne, G. (2010). *W. E. B. Du Bois: A Biography*. Westport, CT: Greenwood Press.
Johnson, B. (2008). *W. E. B. Du Bois: Toward Agnosticism, 1865–1934*. Lanham, MD: Rowman & Littlefield.
Kaestle, C. (1973). *Joseph Lancaster and the Monitorial School Movement*. New York: Teachers College Press.
Kelly-Gangi, C. (2009). *The Essential Wisdom of the Founding Fathers*. New York: Fall River Press.
Kennedy, D. (1980). *Over There: The First World War in American Society*. New York: Oxford University Press.
Ketcham, R. (1984). *Presidents Above Party: The First American Presidency, 1789–1829*. Chapel Hill, NC: University of North Carolina Press. Originally printed in 1902.
Kevles, D. (1985). *In the Name of Eugenics*. Cambridge, MA: Harvard University Press.
Kluger, R. (2004). *Simple Justice: The History of Brown v. Board of Education and Black America's Struggle for Equality*. New York: Vintage Books.
Knoll, M. (2014). "John Dewey as Administrator: The Inglorious End of the Laboratory School in Chicago." *Journal of Curriculum Studies* 47: 203–252.
Lancaster, J. (1803). *Improvements in Education*. London: Darton & Harvey.
Lancaster, J. (1833). *The Epitome of the Chief Events and Transactions of My Own Life*. New Haven, CT: n.p.
Lee, G. C., ed. (1961). *Crusade against Ignorance*. New York: Teachers College Press.
Lewis, D. L. (1993). *W. E. B. Du Bois: A Biography of a Race, 1868–1919*. New York: Henry Holt & Co.
Lewis, D. L. (2009). *W. E. B. Du Bois: The Fight for Equality and the American Century, 1919–1963*. New York: Holt Paperbacks.
Locke, J. (1968). *Some Thoughts Concerning Education in the Educational Writings of John Locke*. Edited by James Axtell, 110–325. Cambridge: Cambridge University Press. Originally published in 1705.
Lutz, A. (1964). *Pioneer Educator of American Women*. Boston: Beacon Press.
Machiavelli, N. (2021). *The Prince*. Gloucester, UK: Reader's Library Classics. Originally published in 1532.

Mann, H. (1846). *Report of the Educational Tour in Germany*. London: n.p.
Mann, M. B. (1937). *Life of Horace Mann*. Washington, DC: National Education Association.
Martin, J. (2003). *The Education of John Dewey*. New York: Columbia University Press.
McGrew Jaime, C., ed. (2015). *Booker T. Washington and W. E. B. DuBois: Two Speeches and an Essay*. Scotts Valley, CA: Create Space Independent Platform.
McGuffey, W. H. (1982). *McGuffeys Eclectic Readers Series*. Fenton, MI: Mott Media. Originally published in 1836.
Messerli, J. (1972). *Horace Mann: A Biography*. New York: Alfred A. Knopf.
Montessori, M. (2020). *The Montessori Method*. New York: DigiReads.com. Originally published in 1912.
Mosier, R. (1965). *Making the American Mind: Social and Moral Ideas in the McGuffey Readers*. New York: Russell & Russell Publications.
Murphy, M. (1990). *Blackboard Unions: The AFT and the NEA, 1900–1980*. Ithaca, NY: Cornell University Press.
Northend, C. (1853). *The Teacher and the Parent: Treatise upon School Education, Containing Practical Suggestions to Teachers and Parents*. Boston: Jenks, Hickling & Swan.
Page, D. (1867). *Theory and Practice of Teaching*. New York: American Book Co.
Parkerson, D., and J. Parkerson. (2001). *Transitions in American Education: A Social History of Teaching*. New York: Routledge Falmer.
Partridge, L. E. (1883). *Notes of Talks and Teaching Given by Francis W. Parker*. New York: E. L. Kellogg and Company.
Partridge, L. E. (2013). *The Quincy Methods Illustrated*. Book on Demand. Originally published in 1985.
Pecaut, F. (1881). *Educational Writings of Horace Mann*. Boston: Lee & Shepard Publishers.
Plutarch. (1969). *Plutarch's Lives of the Noble Greeks and Romans*. London: Easton Press.
Potter, A. (1842). *The School and the Schoolmaster: A Manual for the Use of Teachers, Employers, Trustees, Inspectors, Etc., of Common Schools, Pt. 1*. New York: Harper & Brothers.
Ray, J. (2001). *Ray's Arithmetic Series*, 8 vols. Fenton, MI: Mott Media.
Reese, J. L. (1827). *A Pocket Manual of the Lancastrian's Method of Education in its Most Improved State as practical in the Modern School*. Philadelphia: n.p.
Reilly, W. E., ed. (1990). *Sarah Jane Foster: Teacher of the Freedmen*. Charlotteville: University of Virginia Press.
Rice, J. M. (1893). *The Public School System of the United States*. New York: Arno Press.
Ricks, T. E. (2020). *First Principles*. New York: HarperCollins.
Rosen, E. (2007). *The Culture of Collaboration*. New York: Red Ape Publishing.
Rousseau, J. (1968). *The Social Contract of Principles of Political Right*. London: Penguin Classics. Originally published in 1762.

Rousseau, J. (1974). *Emile or on Education*. Trans. Barbara Foxley. London: Everyman's Library. Originally published in 1762.
Rudolph, F., ed. (1965). *Essays on Education in the Early Republic*. Cambridge, MA: Harvard University Press.
Rudwick, Elliott. (1969). *The Making of Black America, Vol 2: The Black Community in Black America*. New York: Atheneum.
Ruggles, A. (1950). *The Story of the McGuffeys*. Woodstock, GA: American Book Co.
Salmon, D. (1904). *Joseph Lancaster.* London: Longmans, Green & Co.
Shor, I., and P. Freire. (1987). *A Pedagogy for Liberation*. Westport, CT: Bergin & Garvey.
Shuey, A. (1958). *The Testing of Negro Intelligence*. New York: Social Science Press.
Standing, E. M. (1998). *Maria Montessori: Her Life and Work*. New York: Plume. Originally published in 1957.
Taylor, B. (2010). *Horace Mann's Legacy: The Education of Democratic Citizens*. Lawrence: University Press of Kansas.
Urban, W. (2008). *Black Scholar: Horace Mann Bond, 1904–1972*. Athens: University of Georgia Press.
Vasari, G. (2020). *The Lives of the Artists*. New York: Digireads.com.
Wagoner, J. L. (2004). *Jefferson and Education*. Monticello, VA: Thomas Jefferson Foundation.
Westbrook, R. (1992). "John Dewey and American Democracy." *American Historical Review* 97:3, 919–920.
Westbrook, R. (1993). *John Dewey and American Democracy*. Ithaca, NY: Cornell University Press.
Willard, E. (2019). *An Address to the Public: Particularly to the Members of the Legislature of New York Proposing a Plan for Improving Female Education*. Sydney, Australia: Wentworth Press. Originally published in 1819.
Woody, T. (1920). *Early Quaker Education in Pennsylvania*. New York: Teachers College Press.
Woody, T. (1929). *A History of Women's Education in the United States*. New York: Science Press.

About the Authors

Donald Parkerson is Distinguished Professor of Teaching in the History Department at East Carolina University. He has published seven books on the history of education with his coauthor, Jo Ann Parkerson.

Jo Ann Parkerson is professor emeritus of education at Methodist University. She has taught in public schools and published seven books on the history of education with her coauthor, Donald Parkerson.

www.ingramcontent.com/pod-product-compliance
Lightning Source LLC
Chambersburg PA
CBHW022012300426
44117CB00005B/155